TIPS FOR A SUCCESSFUL

ebay™
BUSINESS

DISCARD

CHECK100

TIPS FOR A SUCCESSFUL

ebay™

BUSINESS

TODD ALEXANDER
Australia's leading eBay expert

Wrightbooks
A Wiley Brand

First published in 2014 by Wrightbooks
an imprint of John Wiley & Sons Australia, Ltd
42 McDougall St, Milton Qld 4064
Office also in Melbourne

Typeset in 11.5/13.5 pt Bembo Std

© Todd Alexander

Check 100™ is pending

The moral rights of the author have been asserted

National Library of Australia Cataloguing-in-Publication data:

Author:	Alexander, Todd, author.
Title:	Check 100: Tips for a Successful eBay Business/Todd Alexander.
ISBN:	9780730308621 (pbk)
	9780730308645 (ebook)
Subjects:	eBay (Firm)
	Internet auctions–Australia.
	Finance, Personal–Australia.
	Electronic commerce–Australia.
	Success in business–Australia.
Dewey Number:	381.177

Cover design by Wiley

Cover Image: Paul Bradbury/Getty Images

Printed in Singapore by C.O.S. Printers Pte Ltd

10 9 8 7 6 5 4 3 2 1

Disclaimer
The material in this publication is of the nature of general comment only, and does not represent professional advice. It is not intended to provide specific guidance for particular circumstances and it should not be relied on as the basis for any decision to take action or not take action on any matter which it covers. Readers should obtain professional advice where appropriate, before making any such decision. To the maximum extent permitted by law, the author and publisher disclaim all responsibility and liability to any person, arising directly or indirectly from any person taking or not taking action based on the information in this publication.

Contents

About the author

Todd Alexander has been working in retail and eCommerce for more than 20 years. He is currently Director of Customer Programs at eBay, where he has worked for the past 12 years. During his time at eBay, Todd has helped thousands of Australians to buy and sell successfully on the site. *Check 100* is his fourth eBay book. His previous eBay titles are *How to Use eBay and PayPal, How to Make Money on eBay* and *The New eBay*, which between them have sold more than 45 000 copies.

Todd is also author of the internet titles *Why Pay Retail? Get Your Business Online Now* and *Everyday Internet at Any Age* as well as the novel *Pictures of Us*. Most of Todd's books have become national bestsellers.

A regular contributor to online magazines, blogs and webcasts, Todd is widely regarded as Australia's leading eBay expert. He has degrees in literature and law from Macquarie University.

In what spare time he can find, Todd runs a vineyard, olive grove and accommodation business in the Hunter Valley wine region of NSW, continues selling successfully on eBay and writes fiction.

Follow Todd on Twitter: @Todd_Alexander

Like Todd's Facebook author page:
www.facebook.com/pages/Todd-Alexander-Author/238364049516271

Visit Todd's website: www.toddalexander.net.au

Introduction

This is *Check 100*—the kind of book small to medium business owners have been asking for. I've been advising businesses for more than 20 years and one concern has been consistently expressed: owners do not have the time to read hundreds of pages or attend week-long courses, nor do they have the resources to pay for an expensive consultant. Owners are too busy running the company...which creates a dilemma: how then can they also find time to improve their business? This is where *Check 100* comes in.

In this book you will find 100 must-do tips to ensure your eBay business is successful. If you have an existing eBay business, these are the steps you must take to improve your chances of profitable success. If you're just starting out, these are the 100 things you must incorporate into your eBay business plan.

I've worked at eBay for more than 12 years and in that time I've met thousands of eBay sellers. The tips I have compiled in *Check 100* have been collected from my years of experience, and from talking with small and medium business owners like you. From the biggest eBay business right down to the smallest, everyone I've met has been eager to share their tips for success, and now they're all compiled here for you to emulate.

You can choose to open this book at any page and implement one or more of the tips you find, or you can start at the beginning and work your way through to the end. No one tip is more important than the next so you don't need to follow the book chronologically. This is the power of *Check 100* — find a tip you can implement quickly and next time you pick up the book, find another. Tick the check box once it's complete. You could set yourself the task of completing one check per day so your entire business is optimised for success within three months, or you might prefer to take your time and complete one check per week. This option gives you a two-year turnaround plan.

Each tip gives clear instructions on how to implement it, why you should implement it and how to measure the impact on your eBay business.

Unlike other books, this one doesn't have a 10-page introduction, a list of background reading or a glossary of thousands of terms. You don't have time for any of that. So what are we waiting for? Let's get into it and take 100 steps towards eBay business success.

Throughout this book, I have used a Google URL (web page address) shortener to make it easier for you to copy the correct characters into your search browser. While all URLs in the book begin with http://goo.gl each one will redirect you to the correct page within the relevant website. It's another way to help you save time when completing your 100 checks.

Wherever you see <u>underlined text</u> throughout this book it refers to a clickable link or button on the eBay or PayPal website.

1

Getting the basics right

✓ CHECKS 1 TO 4
Research your competition

What is it?

Without careful and regular monitoring of your competition, you will quickly fall behind in the battle to attract and retain customers. Do not obsess over your competitors, but instead form a high-level view of who they are, what they do and how well they do it.

Three reasons to do it

Buyers can be fickle. If you don't remain competitive by focusing outwardly from your business, you may lose many buyers before you know why it's happening.

1 Ensure you have a range of products that is popular, fresh and constantly evolving.

2 Make sure you're adding value that buyers expect when it comes to postage costs, returns terms, superior service levels, and professionalism of your brand and listings.

3 Remain competitive on price. Internet shoppers are driven by value and will generally always price compare.

Getting started

Conduct your research on eBay and Google (include some international websites—your buyers do), and use the marketplace research tool Terapeak (www.terapeak.com). It's also worth visiting traditional retailers who sell your product so you know what you're competing with offline. It's strongly advisable to conduct a review of your competitors at least once every three months.

Check 1: Competitor list  **($) Free** **Low**

> Create a list of between five and ten competitors. Include their name, user ID, eBay URL and any further information you can find about them, such as their website URL and physical address.

Check 2: Competitor spreadsheet **($) Free** **Low**

> Create a spreadsheet (in Excel or on paper) with factors you would like to compare against. Consider range, price, postage, returns, warranties, service, listings quality, photo quality, professionalism, business policies, feedback and DSR scores on eBay, and position within an eBay search—be as comprehensive as possible.

Getting it done

Now you've created your spreadsheet, be ultra-objective in comparing your business with those of your competitors. If you find this difficult, ask an impartial friend or colleague to do it for you, but insist they be honest, and don't be offended by the results!

Check 3: Competitor scoring **($) Free** **Medium**

> Complete your spreadsheet by giving each competitor (and your own eBay business) a score out of five for each of the factors you have compared. On the spreadsheet, highlight the three factors where you score the most and the three factors where you score the least.

Check 4: Compete to-do list **($) Free** **Medium**

> Write yourself a 'compete better' to-do list so you can become the best eBay business performer on as many of the low-scoring factors as possible. It's okay if you're not the best at everything, but ensure you improve as much as possible.

> *Tip:* You may wish to use other checks in this book to help create your to-do list.

Detailed costs and time for checks 1 to 4

ⓢ $19.95 to $49.95 per month to subscribe to Terapeak (there is also usually a free trial period).

⏰ 1 to 4 hours to conduct your research on eBay, Google, Terapeak and local shopping centres, and create your list of competitors.

⏰ 1 hour to create your competitive factors spreadsheet.

⏰ 2 to 4 hours to critically appraise each of your competitors and your own business, and to fill in your spreadsheet.

⏰ 1 to 2 hours to write your 'compete better' to-do list (cross-check it against other checks in this book).

Tip: Make sure you restrict yourself to these time limits to avoid spending too much time monitoring your competitors.

Business impact

To gauge potential impact, measure if there's:

⊕ an increase in views (or clicks) to your listings

⊕ an increase in the number of items sold

⊕ an improvement to your position in an eBay search.

More information

■ For more information on Terapeak for eBay go to http://goo.gl/7Tr7gp.

■ Consider the NSW TAFE competitor analysis template at http://goo.gl/eEKp1I.

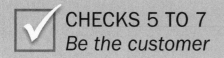

CHECKS 5 TO 7
Be the customer

What is it?

There's no better way to know what your customers are experiencing than by experiencing the same as them firsthand. You can do this in two ways:

1 Ask family or friends to 'mystery-shop' from you then provide a critical appraisal of your service.

2 Purchase regularly from your competitors.

Three reasons to do it

It's a good way of gaining an objective view of what your customers experience when they shop from you, and how your service stacks up against the competition.

1 Quickly highlight the areas of your business that need attention.

2 Learn from your competitors—what can you emulate and what should be avoided?

3 Most buyers will simply leave you if you don't provide the best experience—fix problems before they become irreversible.

Getting started

For this check to be effective you need to act like a typical customer, not expect or demand extraordinary things. If you're selling (and therefore buying) expensive items, you may need to go through the steps of purchase up to, but not including, completing the sale.

Check 5: Competitor list $ Low–Medium Medium

Create a list of five competitors you would like to buy from. Make a note of who they are, what you purchased from them and when. Take notes on how you found the shopping experience. Give each aspect of the experience a score out of five.

Check 6: Mystery shop yourself

 $ Low–Medium Medium

Ask three friends or family members to use a fake name and an address unknown to you to purchase from you. Ask them to make notes about their experience—what they liked, what they didn't like, what was confusing, what was clear. Ask each to give the various aspects of their experience a score out of five.

Tip: If you have no use for the product you have purchased from your competitors, resell it on eBay to recoup some of your costs, or donate it to charity.

Getting it done

Now that you've compiled a list of experiences from your competitors and feedback from people who have purchased from you, it's time to put together an action plan.

Check 7: Action plan for improvement

$ Free Medium

Bring all the feedback together and make a note of the most common positive and negative comments about the experiences provided by your business and those of your competitors. From this, draw up a list of 'emulate' (try to equal or better your competitors in this area) and 'reject' (never provide this type of experience). Create an action plan for when and how you will deliver against these.

Detailed costs and time for checks 5 to 7

(§) Costs will vary depending on how many items you need to purchase and their average price, and whether you pay your friends for their mystery shopping purchases.

(⏱) 1 to 2 hours to complete the necessary purchases.

(⏱) 1 to 2 weeks for you/your mystery shoppers to receive purchases and make an appraisal.

(⏱) 1 to 4 hours to write your 'emulate/reject' list and action plan.

Business impact

To gauge potential impact, measure if there's:

(+) an increase in the number of items sold

(+) an improvement to feedback left by your customers.

More information

To get tips on how to assess your business or that of your competitors, see the ANZ small business mystery shopping guide at http://goo.gl/B2mTTb.

✓ CHECKS 8 AND 9
Optimise for eBay and PayPal fees

What is it?

Both eBay and PayPal have varying fee structures depending on the choices you made when you registered or what you have subscribed to. Changing those choices can help you make significant savings on both sets of fees.

Three reasons to do it

Three reasons probably aren't required for this one because the first one is powerful enough!

1 Optimisation puts more profit in your pocket.

2 Lower fees will enable you to invest those savings in other potential growth areas for your business.

3 Preferable fee rates may enable you to list more products, or different types of products, thereby expanding your range and broadening your appeal to buyers.

Getting started

Before you begin, you need to have a clear idea of your inventory, your listings strategy and the types of categories you list in. Once that's done, visit eBay and PayPal to assess how competitive your current fee rates are.

Getting it done

Remember to revisit your eBay and PayPal subscription/account levels every three to six months, or whenever fees are changed, to ensure you are receiving the best fee rates.

Check 8: Assess eBay fees

On eBay, use the Fee Illustrator to compare the various store packages and estimate which one is the most cost-effective for your business, and the types of listings you create. Go to http://goo.gl/syhmZQ and enter your details. If you need to open a store or change your store level to receive better fee rates, visit the eBay Stores page at http://goo.gl/XRqewV.

Check 9: Assess PayPal fees

On PayPal, there are two ways to optimise your fee rates. Firstly, you need to have the right level of account. PayPal charges different types of fees for different types of transactions. To view each account type and to upgrade your PayPal account, log into PayPal at www.paypal.com.au. Once you're registered with PayPal, if your monthly sales exceed $5000 you can automatically receive a reduced fee rate. You need to apply for PayPal's merchant rates only once and if you qualify, the new fee rate will automatically be charged. Go to http://goo.gl/1ln9JJ to apply.

Detailed costs and time for checks 8 and 9

About 15 minutes to use eBay's Fee Illustrator to get a fast estimate of the best fees package for your store.

Less than 5 minutes to open an eBay store or upgrade to a new level. Note that you may need to place a credit card on file with eBay to upgrade or open a store—follow the prompts to make your credit card your default bill payment method, then once your store is opened or upgraded, change your default bill payment method to whichever you prefer.

A monthly subscription fee of between $19.95 and $499.95 will be charged depending on which eBay store level you require, but change your store level only if it results in a total reduction in percentage of fees paid.

⊕ Less than 5 minutes to change your PayPal account type—it costs nothing to do so though your total fees paid may be affected.

⊕ Less than 5 minutes to register for PayPal's preferred merchant rates, and it costs you nothing.

Business impact

To gauge potential impact, measure if there's:

⊝ a decrease in the total eBay and PayPal fees paid—ensure you measure this as a percentage of total sales to take into account seasonal fluctuations in your sales levels.

More information

■ For a complete list of eBay's fees go to http://goo.gl/7llFvh.

■ For a complete list of PayPal's fees go to http://goo.gl/a5KRQj.

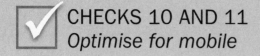

CHECKS 10 AND 11
Optimise for mobile

What is it?

eBay has made a significant investment in its global mobile strategy. Today a high percentage of eBay shoppers are using their mobile to search for and purchase products. The way your business appears on a desktop may be different from the way buyers see it on mobile and via eBay apps, so it's critical to ensure your products are presented in the best possible way to the most possible buyers.

Three reasons to do it

Mobile commerce will continue to be a crucial growth strategy for eBay and other companies. In the future it has been predicted that desktops may disappear altogether, and even within the next two to three years more eBay buyers will purchase via mobile than desktop.

1 Ensure your products are presented to every type of buyer.

2 Optimise your eBay listings for mobile so you don't have to invest in a mobile strategy of your own.

3 Pre-empt future trends by updating your listings today.

Getting started

Different screens and devices display the same information differently. To see how your listings appear to a wide range of customers, you need to see them firsthand. Ask your friends, family and colleagues if you can borrow a range of devices and view one identical listing across each to gauge whether they are all optimised for that screen.

Check 10: Device research *Free* *Medium*

In your research, you should consider:

- desktop computers—use a number of different internet browsers including Internet Explorer, Firefox and Chrome
- Apple iPhone & iPod Touch
- Apple iPad
- Android
- Windows phone
- BlackBerry.

For each device use both the eBay app and mobile web (or mweb) (by typing www.eBay.com.au into the relevant internet browser).

Getting it done

Identify any component of your listings that needs to be updated to ensure they are all optimised for as many devices as possible.

Check 11: Optimise listings *Free* *Medium–High*

Bulk edit your listings on eBay to save you time. To make the necessary adjustments, go to http://goo.gl/IcFJXm.

Detailed costs and time for checks 10 and 11

🕑 💲 1 to 3 hours to view your listings across each of the various devices. eBay apps are free to download.

🕑 💲 1 to 5 hours to update your listings depending on how complex the changes are and how many listings you have, but it's worth spending this time. It should cost you no additional fees to upgrade basic listing information and your design templates.

Business impact

To gauge potential impact, measure if there's:

⊖ a decrease in the number of questions received from buyers

⊕ an improvement in conversion (the number of item views per listing that convert to purchases).

More information

The Queensland government has a basic guide on how businesses can optimise for mobile at http://goo.gl/NVIVSC.

2

Business planning and automation

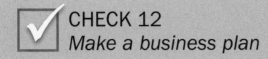

CHECK 12
Make a business plan

What is it?

A business plan is essentially a record that summarises everything about your business. The right plan helps business owners consider all aspects of running a successful and profitable business, such as management, sourcing, customer service, budgeting and finance, and growth. Creating an effective plan takes a lot of energy, commitment and time, but imagine building a house without a plan.

Three reasons to do it

Not having a business plan will lead to inefficiencies in your operations and may mean you lose sight of the big picture.

1   Set yourself clear targets so you can track your business's progress.

2   Create a written record of your business information, suppliers, inventory, staff and all other components of running your business.

3   Ensure you stay on top of all the administration involved in running a successful business.

Getting started

Before you begin, make sure you have all the relevant information within easy reach. It's sensible to create your plan on computer so you can easily update it, insert information when and as required, and complete any additional research via the internet. Allow yourself plenty of time and space—you will need to concentrate and complete the plan thoroughly.

Getting it done

It's important you complete as many sections of your business plan as possible. The document should evolve over time, and some information will need to be added at a later date. Remember to keep your business plan fresh—update it frequently and return to it often to ensure you are on track to meet your targets.

Check 12: Create a business plan    *Free* *High*

Conduct an internet search for 'business plan template' and download the one that best suits your needs. Though not specific to online or eBay, the Australian government's free template at http://goo.gl/gsqVfV is recommended. Add sections to tailor any template to your business's needs. Complete the template and save it in a safe place on your computer. Set yourself a reminder to review your plan regularly.

Tip: It's a good idea to share your business plan with a mentor, a business adviser or someone you trust to give you sound professional advice. Save a second copy of your plan on a USB (or disk) and keep it in a safe place away from your computer.

Detailed costs and time for check 12

⊕ ⑤ 3 hours to 2 days to comprehensively complete your business plan. You can download a lot of business plan templates free from the internet.

⊕ 1 to 2 hours every month to revisit, update and add to your plan.

Business impact

It may be harder for you to directly measure the impact a business plan has on your business but a good plan will lead to:

⊕ an increase in business efficiencies (sourcing, profit calculations, staffing, goal setting).

More information

Visit the Australian government's www. business.gov.au website for guides and business planning tools at http://goo.gl/iNhefl.

✓ CHECK 13
Create a profit and loss spreadsheet

What is it?

A profit and loss spreadsheet lists every single expense associated with running your business, and every single form of income. Tallying the two allows you to assess your gross income (total sales) and your net income (total sales minus total costs). Your profit margin is net income as a percentage of gross income.

Three reasons to do it

Without a comprehensive profit and loss spreadsheet you will have no idea exactly how much profit you are making and therefore how viable your business may be.

1   Easily keep track of all your expenses and income, which can help with tax returns and GST statements (if you complete them).

2   Gauge your profit margin at any given point in time so you can adjust expenses to ensure you maintain a set level of profit.

3   Keeping track of expenses makes it easier for you to compare different service providers to ensure you are always getting the best rates available.

Getting started

While you can create a profit and loss spreadsheet on a piece of paper, it's more sensible to use an accounting application such as Excel or Numbers, or within an existing accounting software package such as MYOB, which offers 'live' or up-to-the-minute reporting. Other profit and loss templates are available for download from the internet.

Getting it done

It's important to be as comprehensive as possible and include every conceivable cost and source of income for your eBay business. Create a list for each month of the year, and tally months into quarterly statements (this will help if you need to create a quarterly business activity statement (BAS) for the tax office) and into each financial year (July 1 to June 30). For each entry, add columns for GST amount paid/received, capital or usual expense (essential for BAS—a capital expense is usually a piece of equipment that costs more than $1500), date and a notes column (to add specific details). Keep all related receipts in month and date order to assist with accurate and faster bookkeeping.

Check 13: Profit and loss report

$ Free   **Medium**

You need to create two lists for a profit and loss report. Start with the costs of running your business, including (but not limited to):

- eBay fees
- PayPal fees
- credit card processing fees
- other costs, such as bank fees
- cost of goods purchased
- any taxes or duties paid on goods purchased
- postage
- packaging
- stationery (thank you notes, letterheads, business cards and so on)

- office supplies (paper, scissors, knives, tape dispensers, folders, filing systems, printer ink, pens, notepads and so on)

- hardware, such as computer, printer, desk, chair

- telephone/fax

- internet service

- third-party fees (designers, listing tools and so on)

- accountant

- lawyer/business adviser

- software

- electricity, gas, water

- storage/warehousing organisation

- additional resources (books, magazines, subscriptions and so on)

- petrol/travel costs (trips to the post office, to meet suppliers and so on)

- rent (including a portion of your mortgage relevant to the percentage of your home used in operating the business, if applicable)

- insurance

- cost of refunds, and replaced or damaged products

- staff costs

- GST/tax

- advertising and marketing.

Next create a list of all income, including:

- eBay sales

- postage paid by buyers

- additional fees paid by buyers (registered mail, extended warranty and so on)
- additional sales
- resale of any equipment or goods used in running your business.

Detailed costs and time for check 13

⊕ 3 to 5 hours to create your monthly template and label all fields according to your business's needs.

⊕ 3 to 5 hours per month to complete your spreadsheet, depending on the size of your business.

Business impact

An accurate and current profit and loss report will allow you to adjust costs to help you:

⊕ improve profit

⊖ reduce time spent on administrative tasks and completing monthly, quarterly and yearly reporting.

More information

Visit the Australian government's www.business.gov.au website for more information about profit and loss reports at http://goo.gl/e4qOAX.

✓ CHECKS 14 AND 15
Create business policies

What is it?

Business policies are an eBay shortcut that allow you to apply the same types of policies across all or similar types of your eBay listings. They include such things as returns policies, handling time, payments and postage policies. Opting into the program is gradual, and when you qualify you will see a notice within My eBay.

Three reasons to do it

More than anything else, using eBay's business policies will save you a lot of time, now and in the future.

1 Ensure consistency of policies across your listings so buyers know what to expect every time they buy from you.

2 Utilising business policies makes it easier for you to update all of your listings at once, instead of having to do them one at a time.

3 Mix and match your policies by different listing or product types to ensure you're offering the best possible service to your buyers.

Getting started

Before you begin arbitrarily applying your proposed set of business policies, it's vital to ensure that they are competitive within your category.

Check 14: Compare competitors' policies

 **Free** **Low**

Take a look at the policies offered by your main competitors and assess how you can offer the same, or perhaps better.

Getting it done

If you've created a comprehensive business plan, you should have a list of your products for sale. Within your business plan, or by creating a new list, group your products into similar types and assign your business policies against each product type.

Check 15: Create your policies    **Free** **Low**

Using eBay's Business Policies functionality, assign your business policies against each product type. Complete instructions for how to update, amend and cancel your business policies can be found at http://goo.gl/Qu9ONf.

Detailed costs and time for checks 14 and 15

- ⏰ $ 1 to 2 hours and free to assess the policies offered by your competitors.

- ⏰ $ 1 to 4 hours and free to update your business policies using eBay's editing tool.

Business impact

To gauge potential impact, measure if there's:

⊖ a decrease in the number of questions asked by your buyers

⊕ an improvement in the ratings left by buyers.

More information

See eBay's business policies page at http://goo.gl/HFxDc7.

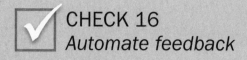

CHECK 16
Automate feedback

What is it?

Every time one of your buyers pays for a product you should leave them professional, polite and branded feedback. Consider a message such as 'Thank you for choosing to buy your [insert product type] from [insert your eBay name]'. Rather than manually leaving feedback for each transaction, you can choose to automatically leave random feedback comments for your buyers as soon as they have paid.

Three reasons to do it

Automating as much of your eBay business as possible means less time spent completing basic administration tasks.

1 Automation saves time and effort.

2 It ensures your buyers always receive feedback the moment their payment has been received, encouraging a positive trading relationship and creating a professional impression.

3 By carefully entering your list of random feedback comments you can be assured that they will be consistent, branded and error free, thereby creating a more professional brand image for your customers.

Getting started

A note about feedback. Feedback was originally utilised by eBay to help create a more transparent marketplace for buyers and sellers alike. Over the years the system has evolved considerably, including removal of the ability for sellers to leave their buyers negative feedback. It's important to concentrate on the bigger picture — yes, feedback is an indicator of your eBay reputation, but it's just one of many factors buyers assess before choosing who to purchase from. What's important is that you remain objective about your listings and ensure you have removed as many points of confusion or annoyance as possible. If you receive negative feedback, learn from your experience and adjust your business accordingly. Multiple negative ratings are an alert that you may need to make more systemic changes to the way you do business.

You need to ensure your feedback score is comparable to those of other sellers within your category, and remember that your overall seller reputation (feedback, detailed seller ratings, the number of disputes lodged against you by buyers) is just one factor for determining your listing's visibility on the search results page.

You will need to be subscribed to Selling Manager in order to automate your feedback preferences. To subscribe go to http://goo.gl/4o26fL.

Getting it done

Sellers who leave their buyers positive, professional and branded feedback as soon as they have paid are setting a positive tone for the transaction.

Check 16: Automate feedback  Free Low

In My eBay under Selling Manager on the left, click Automation Preferences. Check the 'Automatically leave the following positive feedback' box and choose your preferred option. Click Edit stored comments to update your random comments. Follow complete instructions at http://goo.gl/PloQCJ.

Tip: Ask a colleague or friend to check it carefully, or cut and paste your comments into a spellchecker to ensure that you make no errors.

Detailed costs and time for check 16

⑤ $9.95 per month to subscribe to Selling Manager Pro (free if you subscribe to an eBay store).

⊕ 30 to 60 minutes to create your feedback and set up automation.

Business impact

To gauge potential impact, measure if there's:

⊕ an increase in the number of positive feedback ratings left by your buyers.

More information

To read all about feedback go to http://goo.gl/o3fzXV.

CHECK 17
Automate unpaid items

What is it?

From time to time, some customers may complete checkout on eBay but then fail to pay for the item. eBay needs to be made aware of when this occurs as it has policies for buyers who fail to pay for their purchase. More importantly, unless you advise eBay that your buyer has failed to pay, you will be charged final value fees on the transaction. Lodging an unpaid item claim is the only way to ensure eBay monitors buyers who consistently fail to pay, and the only way to secure a refund on your final value fees.

Three reasons to do it

Staying on top of unpaid items can be troublesome if you sell hundreds or thousands of items each week. You need to remind buyers to pay, but you also need to advise eBay when they fail to respond to the reminders. Automating the process means you never have to manually complete an unpaid item claim.

1 Save time on administration tasks.

2 Secure your final value fee refund on all unpaid items automatically.

3 Help keep the eBay marketplace safe and fair by ensuring that eBay is alerted to buyers who consistently fail to pay for their purchases.

Getting started

It's important to note that eBay has a policy against sellers who abuse the unpaid item process. This can lead to a reversal of credits or even suspension. Using the automated process means that only qualifying items will be included. For more information on abuse of the policy go to http://goo.gl/V0hXRe.

Getting it done

Once you've created the automated process, qualifying final value fees will automatically be credited to your eBay account.

Check 17: Automate unpaid items 〔$〕 *Free* 〔🕐〕 *Low*

In the Accounts tab within <u>My eBay</u> click <u>Site Preferences</u>, click <u>Show</u> to the right of Unpaid Item Assistant then click <u>Edit</u>. Select 'Yes I want Unpaid Item Assistant to open and close cases on my behalf', then in the drop-down menu select the number of days you want Unpaid Item Assistant to wait before opening a case.

Detailed costs and time for check 17

🕐 $ 5 to 10 minutes and free to set up automated Unpaid Item Assistant.

Business impact

To gauge potential impact, measure if there's:

⊖ a reduction of instances where final value fees are charged after the buyer has not paid for the item.

More information

Follow the complete instructions for Unpaid Item Assistant at http://goo.gl/TiXLhx.

CHECKS 18 AND 19
Automated inventory management

What is it?

Once you have listed your inventory on eBay, it can take a lot of time to manually keep track of how many products you have listed, how many you have remaining for sale and how many you have left in your warehouse yet to be listed. Accurate and efficient inventory management is a critical component of running a successful eBay business.

Three reasons to do it

The less time you spend manually assessing your stock levels, the more time you will have to invest in other aspects of running your business, such as improving service levels or securing better deals from your suppliers.

1 Stay on top of reordering products by creating alerts when your stock levels are low.

2 Avoid listing more stock than you have available, which can lead to disappointing buyer experiences that may result in your receiving negative ratings.

3 Save time by carefully managing your inventory levels and maximising your cash flow so you reorder stock only when absolutely necessary.

Getting started

Subscribe to Selling Manager Pro to gain access to the inventory management tool. You can subscribe at http://goo.gl/4o26fL.

☑ Check 18: Conduct a stocktake

$ Low   🕐 *Medium–High*

Before you begin, it's a good idea to conduct a stocktake of all of your inventory so you can be sure that the numbers you enter into eBay are accurate. Your business plan should contain a list of all of your products for sale, and a well-organised warehouse means you should be able to count stock figures effectively. Update your Stock on Hand figures after you have completed your stocktake.

Getting it done

Now you have your updated stock figures, use Selling Manager Pro to update your Total on Hand numbers. This total is independent of how many transactions you have associated with pending, active or unsent. The inventory system will allow you to relist, create stock alerts when your levels are low, and make a record of other information such as cost price, supplier details and where they are located within your warehouse.

☑ Check 19: Update eBay inventory

$ Free   🕐 *Medium–High*

Within My eBay under Selling Manager Pro on the left, click Inventory then click the Create Product button. Complete the relevant product information then click Create Listing. Alternatively, for existing listings, click Active under Selling Manager Pro, check the box next to the relevant listing then use the drop-down next to Action to click Save to inventory. Complete the relevant product information then click Save to inventory.

Once you have created your products within your inventory, you can then update all of the specific information outlined above, including alerts. For complete instructions go to http://goo.gl/JPQo3j.

Tip: Third-party providers also supply inventory management systems that allow you to accurately assess your stock levels, set alerts and automate rules. The prices and types of service available vary. You can compare some of the services at http://goo.gl/qXaKV9.

Detailed costs and time for checks 18 and 19

🕐 1 to 6 hours to complete a product stocktake (longer for larger businesses).

🕐 5 to 15 minutes per product to create a new product template within Selling Manager Pro.

🕐 1 to 5 minutes per product to save active listings to your product inventory.

⑧ $9.95 per month to subscribe to Selling Manager Pro (free if you subscribe to an eBay store).

Business impact

To gauge potential impact, measure if there's:

⊖ a decrease in instances of your products being out of stock

⊕ increased efficiencies in ordering, calculating margins and maintaining supplier relations

⊖ a decrease in the time spent manually managing your inventory levels, eBay listings and relistings.

More information

A complete outline of Selling Manager Pro can be found at http://goo.gl/PJTwxL.

3

Sourcing and listing products

✓ CHECK 20
Create a target list of products

What is it?

Whether you have zero or 10000 products currently for sale on eBay, you need to have a list of additional products you would like to source for sale on the site. Circumstances can change in an instant, requiring you to expand your range, change suppliers or move into a completely new category. For example, a sudden influx in highly competitive sellers may render selling a particular product unprofitable; one of your suppliers could go out of business or change their terms of trade so that buying from them is no longer tenable; or you may find yourself with additional funds that could be reinvested into the business by sourcing additional products to sell. In each of these (and many other) circumstances, you may be required to source supply quickly.

Three reasons to do it

1   Having a ready-made list of potential suppliers and their products will mean that you are ready to expand or change your inventory with minimal notice.

2   Create a wish list of products to help you realise goals within your business. For example, in year three I would like to have 10000 products listed including x, y and z. Without goals you are unlikely to plan adequately for your business's growth.

3   Keep your list of suppliers and products within your categories current so you can stay abreast of pricing, sourcing and range trends.

Getting started

Most of the information you will need will be available via the internet. Look for keywords such as *manufacturer, supplier, wholesaler, importer* and *exporter*. Do not assume that all the suppliers you need will be located within Australia—in fact, locating an overseas supplier could mean higher profit margins for you. You may need to visit bricks-and-mortar stores or businesses to better gauge product quality, and remember that the products themselves often include information about the manufacturer or supplier.

Getting it done

Your target list of products (and suppliers) should be as comprehensive as possible and contain all the relevant information you need to make informed decisions about who you should be buying from, what range you should be stocking and when. Most of this information should be included in your business plan and can form the foundation for your eBay listing descriptions. Where possible, ask for samples of the products to ensure they are of the right quality.

Check 20: Create a target product list

$ Free   Low–Medium

Create a spreadsheet for your product list. Your column headings should be:

- Category
- Product Name
- Product Number
- Product Description (dimensions, materials and so on)
- Product Photograph

- Package Quantity
- Minimum Order Quantity
- Cost
- Delivery Cost
- Other Costs (taxes, duties and so on)
- Lead Time
- Supplier
- Contact Name
- Address
- Telephone
- Email
- Website
- Other Contact Details
- Terms of Trade (payment terms, returns and so on)
- Average eBay Sold Price
- Forecast Monthly eBay Sales
- List of eBay Sellers.

Detailed costs and time for check 20

⊕ 10 to 60 minutes for each product type to compile all the relevant information.

⊕ 1 day to several weeks to receive product samples.

⑤ Suppliers may charge for samples and/or postage costs.

Business impact

Creating a thorough and extensive list of potential products can lead to business efficiencies such as:

- ⊖ reductions in time taken to place and receive orders
- ⊖ a reduction in time taken to list products on eBay (copy and paste existing information into your templates)
- ⊕ faster reaction times to external pressures such as change in suppliers, price competition or lack of supply.

More information

The Queensland government has a great guide to finding suppliers at http://goo.gl/0ul1AF.

✓ CHECKS 21 AND 22
Create a supplier pitch

What is it?

While you may already have suppliers in place, as you expand your range, or perhaps when a supplier is no longer able to supply your products, you may be required to approach more suppliers. Not all suppliers will automatically accept you as a potential reseller. Most larger businesses want to retain control over their brand, which means influencing how their products are presented and which channels they're sold through. Having a template for a supplier pitch means you will be able to approach any company, any time, with a convincing argument for why you should become one of their resellers.

Three reasons to do it

Having a ready-made pitch document means you will be prepared for supplier communications at any given time.

1 Having a prepared pitch document means you will have had time to polish it, reducing potential for errors and increasing the likelihood that you know the content well and can answer questions or concerns more confidently.

2 A supplier pitch helps you refine your own brand—what your business stands for, who your target customers are and what kinds of products you would like to sell.

3 Stay current with a list of eBay trends and keep your pitch document updated. A highly polished and professional pitch can mean the difference between you or someone else becoming the reseller of a product, and could also lead to exclusivity arrangements.

Getting started

Your pitch needs to be in a format you're comfortable presenting in, but also one that is easily viewed by a wide variety of potential suppliers. PowerPoint, or a similar presentation application, is probably the most commonly used format. You could also consider printed and bound booklets, video or other more tactile formats, but better to choose one that can be quickly updated and use a template that allows you to slot in relevant information.

Check 21: Find or create a pitch template

$ *Free–Low*   **Low**

Start by creating or finding a template that you're comfortable with. You can download a free one via the internet or create your own. The template should clearly reflect your brand, be simple yet striking and be carefully pitched at the right level of decision-maker. For example, if you intend to pitch to the CEO you may need your information to be more concise, whereas an accountant or business development manager may want to see more granular information. A good template will allow you to create and edit multiple versions as you go.

Getting it done

Once you've created or located a pitch template you're comfortable with, the next step is to fill in the various parts in a way that engages and convinces all potential suppliers. Avoid lengthy details around your negotiable terms, such as cost of purchase and delivery. The pitch document should be about convincing the supplier that (a) there is a complementary market for their product on eBay and (b) yours is the right business to be reselling it.

Check 22: Write the pitch   *Free*   *Low–Medium*

Complete the relevant fields within your pitch by concentrating on one supplier and one product type. These should include:

- a brief description of who you are

- a history of your business and its success (particularly on eBay)

- a comprehensive summary of the category/industry and its current challenges and successes

- data around current eBay trends for the category/product

- an outline of the sales potential on eBay complete with forecast and timeline

- an example of how you think the product/brand should be positioned on eBay

- a checklist of how the relationship between the supplier and you as reseller will work

- next steps—a complete timeline of what should be decided when and by whom.

Tip: Practise presenting your pitch to a range of colleagues and friends, and be receptive to their feedback. Ask for a critical appraisal and look particularly for inaccuracies. Always remember to carefully check every tiny aspect of your pitch when you update it for a new supplier or product—the last thing you want is the supplier thinking you're too lazy to update it for their business.

Detailed costs and time for checks 21 and 22

⏱ ⑤ 1 to 3 hours to create your own pitch template from scratch or locate a great one on the internet. Some downloadable templates need to be paid for.

⏱ 1 to 3 hours to populate the template with the relevant information for each new supplier.

Business impact

To gauge potential impact, measure if there's:

⊕ an increase in the number of suppliers who allow you to resell their product

⊕ an increase in the number of products you list on eBay

⊕ an increase in the number of items sold.

More information

For inspiration visit Board of Innovation at http://goo.gl/h8r4KY.

CHECKS 23 AND 24
Improve your titles

What is it?

There is no such thing as the perfect title. This means there is always room for improvement! Your titles need to be the best they can be, when compared with competitors in your category, and bearing in mind how buyers look for products such as the ones you sell. Furthermore, you need to stay informed of eBay's changes to how your listing titles are referenced within eBay searches, because often your placement in search results relates directly to the quality and accuracy of your listing titles.

Three reasons to do it

Next to photographs and price, item titles are among the most important things your buyers look at when assessing whether to click through to your eBay listing and purchase from you or one of your competitors.

1   Great titles result in a better placement in search results.

2   Current and optimised titles will attract more buyer attention — avoid filling valuable title space with redundant characters.

3   Skilful titles may attract more clicks from potential buyers and provide you with a competitive advantage.

Getting started

The best listing titles need to be highly relevant, respond to buyer needs and be optimised for eBay's search system.

Check 23: Compare competitors' titles

(\$) *Free*   (🕐) *Low–Medium*

Start by looking at your competitors, both on and off eBay, and make a list of the top 10 and worst 10 titles across three of your key products. In your opinion, what makes a great title and what makes a bad one? Make some notes on how you think your listing titles could be stronger.

Getting it done

If you already have a sales history from your listing you will not be able to edit your listing title on eBay. You need to make a judgement on whether you think updating your listing titles by creating new listings will be worthwhile. Bear in mind that one of the most influential factors for determining your visibility in an eBay search result is your recent sales history, and how frequently buyers have clicked on or watched your listing. In some cases, creating a new listing with a formidable title can result in a superior position within an eBay search. If you're unsure, test this in a handful of listings to gauge whether the new title drives greater success.

Consider the following factors when creating your listing title:

- Choose relevant keywords relating to your product. Use as many keywords as you can and include as many product features as you can think of, such as brand, size, colour and materials.

- Occasion-related keywords may also be helpful (such as 'novelty' or 'wedding').

- Avoid repeating the same word, even if it makes your listing title less grammatically correct. For example, 'wedding dress party dress formal dress' in your title includes two redundant uses of the word *dress* when it comes to how eBay's search references your listings. Instead, consider 'wedding party formal dress'.

- Avoid only loosely associated keywords. This will mean your listing receives impressions for broad keywords not applicable to buyers and may result in your popularity score within Best Match being negatively affected. For example, if you use the words 'garden, gardening' when selling seeds, the chances of a buyer searching for a broad keyword when they really want a packet of seeds is small; and similarly, anyone searching 'garden' is unlikely to click through to your listing for seeds.

- Avoid keyword spamming—using words not directly applicable to your listing. For example, if selling seeds, don't use a title such as 'strawberry seeds jam sauce'. While you may grow seeds into a plant that can be used to make jam and sauce, you're not selling jam or sauce so you should not use these keywords. For more on eBay's strict policy against keyword spamming go to http://goo.gl/qGgk4V.

- A good example will include strong keywords, such as: 'Brand New Size 32 Waist 33 Leg Men's Black Diesel Faded Denim Jeans Slim Fit'.

Check 24: Update or create listing titles

$ Free–Low   ⏱ Medium–High

To update your titles for listings with no sales history go to <u>My eBay</u>, click <u>Active</u> under Selling Manager Pro, check the box next to the relevant listing(s) then, using the drop-down next to <u>Edit</u>, click <u>Edit selected</u> or <u>Edit all</u>. On the next screen check the box at the top of the page to highlight all listings then, using the drop-down next to <u>Edit</u>, click <u>Title and subtitle</u> then select <u>Edit listings individually</u>. Make your changes then click <u>Save and close</u>. Alternatively you can double-click on the title column to make your changes directly on the page.

To edit listings with a sales history you will need to end your listings by going to <u>My eBay</u>, clicking <u>Active</u> under Selling Manager Pro, then checking the box next to the relevant listing(s), then using the drop-down next to <u>Action</u> click <u>End</u>. Once ended, click <u>Unsold</u> under Selling Manager Pro, update your listing titles as per the above then relist your listings.

Detailed costs and time for checks 23 and 24

⏱ 1 to 2 hours to research and compare great and bad listing titles.

⏱ 1 to 2 minutes per listing to create optimised listing titles.

⑤ Ended listings will need to be relisted, which may attract an additional insertion fee.

Business impact

To gauge potential impact, measure if there's:

⊕ an increase in views (or clicks) to your listings

⊕ an increase in the number of items sold

⊕ an improvement to your position in an eBay search.

More information

For more on bulk edit see http://goo.gl/8dIviq.

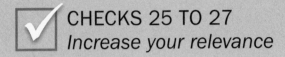

CHECKS 25 TO 27
Increase your relevance

What is it?

Appearing higher up in eBay's search results depends on much more than just your listing title. In order to maximise your chances of being first in any search result, you need to attract the most buyer attention, and also to ensure eBay can read your listing as being relevant for any given buyer search. You do this by utilising features such as choosing the most accurate category and eBay's item specifics or product attributes.

Three reasons to do it

Relevance is a critical determining factor in where your listing appears in eBay search results, and for some buyers it can make the difference between finding your listing and never seeing it at all.

1   It will increase your chances of appearing higher up in search results.

2   For buyers who use refinements after they search, using the most accurate attributes will help ensure your products are found.

3   Using the right features may mean your listings are shown in more types of buyer searches.

Getting started

Before you begin, conduct a quick comparison of your listings and those of your main competitors. While this will take a little time, it's important to ensure that you are maximising relevance for your particular category rather than making assumptions about what your buyers want.

Check 25: Compare competitors' listings

 **$** *Free* **🕐** *Low–Medium*

Make a list of your top 10 products and the categories and item specifics you have chosen. Next, find three to five sellers of the same (or similar) products and note the categories and item specifics they have chosen. Pay particular attention to any listing that appears higher than yours in search results. Once you've created your list, look for where your details are different, and how they might be improved. Remember to think objectively and put yourself in your buyers' shoes.

Tip: You can also use the third-party research tool Terapeak at www.terapeak.com to view the most popular categories used by sellers and top-performing listings.

Getting it done

The two main areas to concentrate on are your use of category and of item specifics.

Check 26: Category update   **$** *Free*   **🕐** *Low–Medium*

Update your categories by completing a bulk inventory edit, as detailed in check 19. Avoid using categories called 'Other' as these are generally used only when there isn't a more accurate category to use. Buyers tend to avoid filtering by these categories. It's also important to stay up to date with category changes made by eBay—visit http://goo.gl/Vibljj and look for 'Seller Release' announcements.

Check 27: Item specifics update

$ Free   Low–Medium

Update your item specifics by completing a bulk inventory edit, as detailed in check 19. Item specifics are also a critical component of determining whether your listing is relevant to any given buyer's search. Where they are available, you should *always* use them. Buyers often narrow their searches using filters, and many of these are populated by a seller's use of item specifics. It's crucial to use them properly: enter single values only, and do not use redundant words.

Correct use	Incorrect use
Blue	Blue & Red
Blue	Blue with Red Dots
Hen's Night	Hen's Night Party
Green	Lime Colour
Unisex	Boys, Girls

Detailed costs and time for checks 25 to 27

$ $19.95 to $49.95 per month to subscribe to Terapeak — there is also usually a free trial period.

🕑 1 to 3 hours to research comparable listings on eBay.

🕑 1 to 10 minutes per listing to update — faster if you use bulk edit.

Business impact

To gauge potential impact, measure if there's:

⊕ an increase in views (or clicks) to your listings

⊕ an increase in the number of items sold

⊕ an improvement in your position in an eBay search.

More information

- For more information on item specifics go to
  http://goo.gl/B2KLOZ.

- For more information on choosing categories go to
  http://goo.gl/e3Imcd.

CHECKS 28 TO 30
Optimise for Best Match

What is it?

Best Match is eBay's default search order. It is a complex set of algorithms that are constantly changing. The simplest way to think about Best Match is that your listing's visibility is a combination of the following factors:

- *buyer engagement:* how many times your listing is viewed or clicked, how many buyers watch your item, and how many times you sell a product from your listing or a bid is placed on an auction

- *relevance:* a combination of the words you use in your listing title and use of features such as category selection and product attributes (see checks 25 to 27)

- *seller performance:* how your history as a seller compares with others in your category (as measured by your feedback score, detailed seller ratings and your compliance with all of eBay's policies).

Three reasons to do it

You can have the best product and offer the best service in the world, but unless your visibility is optimised for eBay searches your listings may never be seen. Being optimised for Best Match can make a critical difference to your business's turnover.

1   Increase your chances of appearing higher up in eBay's search results.

2 Ensure your complete product offering is highly competitive against those of other sellers in your category.

3 Ensure your listings appeal to as many buyers as possible to improve your search-to-purchase ratio.

Getting started

Used in conjunction with checks 23 to 27, it's important to remember a few additional details about how Best Match operates.

- For any given search result, it compares your performance versus other sellers and listings.

- Many factors lead a buyer to choose to engage with your listing. You need to remain competitive on a range of details including item price, postage costs, postage services, handling time, quality of item photograph, quality of item title and description, and your terms of trade such as payments and returns. It's crucial that you compare your experience objectively with that of other sellers in your category.

- If your position in search changes, don't automatically assume that the algorithm has changed. While it's true the algorithm is being continually refined, it is largely determined by buyer behaviour. A change in your position is most likely directly related to a change by your competitors.

Getting it done

Optimising your listing title and the relevance factors of your listing (such as category and item specifics) are two ways to improve your visibility in an eBay search result. The following three checks are also critical components and you should revisit your performance of each on a regular basis.

Check 28: Update listing duration

$ Free–Low   **Low–Medium**

List in longer duration formats such as Stores' Good Til Cancelled (GTC) 30-day duration. By listing in longer formats, you're optimising your recent sales history (or buyer engagement) and ensuring your listing remains live continually. Any time your listing is not live is a lost opportunity for improving your buyer engagement scores. You need to be subscribed to eBay Stores to access the GTC listing format and you can update your live listings by using the bulk editing tool, as outlined in check 11.

Check 29: Use multi-variant

$ Free–Low   **Low–Medium**

Duration is one way to maximise your exposure on the site, but another way to attract more buyers to your listings and to further boost your buyer engagement scores is to combine similar product types into one listing. Known as multi-variant, this allows you, for example, to have one listing of the same style dress but to include multiple sizes and colours. Rather than having one black size 12 dress in your listing, therefore, your multi-variant listing will appeal to people searching for a black dress in size 8, 10, 12 or 14, or red, blue and white versions of the same style and sizes. You can see that in this way you are increasing your potential buyer base 16-fold. You can upload different photographs for each variation, and each is also cross-referenced by eBay's search even if they are not included within your item title. You can update your listings by following the instructions at http://goo.gl/1I9rpO or use eBay's multi-variation merger tool at http://goo.gl/O1WuwF.

Check 30: Check your performance  Free Low

A final important part of the Best Match algorithm is your seller performance rating. This is a combination of your feedback score, detailed seller ratings, number of disputes lodged against you and eBay policy compliance. To stay current with your seller performance, it's important to check your status on a regular basis. Make yourself a calendar reminder now to check your seller status at least fortnightly. You can view your seller dashboard within <u>My eBay</u>: click <u>Account</u> then <u>Seller Dashboard</u>. If there are issues with your performance you will receive notification here along with tips or actions on how to improve.

Detailed costs and time for checks 28 to 30

⑤ $19.95 to $499.95 per month to subscribe to Stores and access 30-day Good Til Cancelled listings.

⊕ 1 to 3 minutes per listing to update your duration (less if you use eBay's bulk editing tool).

⊕ 1 to 5 minutes to create a multi-variant listing (less if you use eBay's Multi Variation Merger tool).

⊕ 10 minutes each fortnight to check your seller dashboard.

Business impact

To gauge potential impact, measure if there's:

⊕ an improvement to your position in an eBay search

⊕ an increase in views (or clicks) to your listings

⊕ an increase in the number of items sold.

More information

To see my video on understanding Best Match go to http://goo.gl/4BxEoi.

✓ CHECKS 31 TO 33
Create professional listings

What is it?

Online, you're expecting a buyer you have never met to send you money for a product they have never seen. There is a high degree of trust required when selling online. To increase buyer confidence in your products and services, and to provide a competitive edge in your category, you need to create listings that are as professional as possible. So how do you define 'professional'? One way is to imagine your listings are required for a catalogue of the best retailer in the world. Professional listings take account of:

- photograph(s) (see checks 48 to 50)
- the amount and quality of product information
- your postage, payments and returns policies
- the tone of the language you use
- the layout of the listings (including order of information, overall design look and feel, spelling and grammar)
- the services you offer.

Three reasons to do it

Buyers expect professionalism and often choose one seller over another based solely on how professional (or trustworthy) their listings appear.

1 Attract more buyers to your listings.

2 Set clear buyer expectations to avoid disappointment, which can lead to negative ratings.

3   Remain highly competitive by providing outstanding professionalism and service — this can often mean you do not have to be the cheapest in the marketplace to attract more customers.

Getting started

Creating professional listings can be one of the most time-consuming components of optimising your eBay performance, but the time investment will be worth it. As with most elements of measuring your success on eBay, you need to ensure the level of professionalism of your listings is better than that of your competitors. You can certainly outsource the creation of your listings to a design agency or freelancer, and remember that once you have created a base template to use you can simply cut and paste product information into each listing. Consider Frooition (www.frooition.com/au) or Dzine (www.dzine-hub.com) to redesign your listings, or conduct an internet search for other agencies.

Getting it done

Even the best design agencies will require a clearly written brief. You need to create the best possible listings for your buyers, so remain objective. The final results should be as polished as a page from one of the best product catalogues in the world and leave no questions unanswered for your potential buyers.

Check 31: Find a designer

($) *Low–Medium*   (🕐) *Low–Medium*

When choosing a designer or agency it's important to work with the one you feel most comfortable with. Price should be a deciding factor but not the sole one. Make sure you ask to see a range of projects completed by the company or person and submit a full outline of your requirements to receive a complete quote. You could also visit a site such as Freelancer (www.freelancer.com.au) to find a professional designer.

Check 32: Create great descriptions

 **$** *Low–Medium* **🕐** *Low–Medium*

While there's no such thing as perfect, you can strive to get as close to it as possible! Here are the critical components of a great eBay listing description:

- First, include as much information about the product as possible. Consider bullet points of information in order of importance. Stick to the facts, and only after you have listed all of the product's features should you consider including additional information such as uses or other expressive language.

- Include multiple photographs of the product.

- List the payment methods you accept.

- Outline your postage services and the cost of each.

- Outline your handling time to give buyers a clear indication of how long it will take for the product to leave your premises.

- Provide a thorough returns policy that gives buyers peace of mind.

- List your contact details clearly.

- Use a consistent, simple, normal-size (at least 10 to 12 point) font, avoiding multiple colours, sizes or styles.

- Left justify your paragraphs—it's easier for people to read.

- Avoid overly expressive or aggressive language.

- Remember to brand your listing professionally to help build buyer confidence.

Check 33: Spellcheck  *Free–Low* *Low–Medium*

Once you have a listing template for one product and are happy with it, it's time to review every single listing to ensure there are no spelling mistakes. These can deter some buyers and make your brand look unprofessional. Ask someone with impeccable spelling to check your listings or else run them through a spellchecker. Though this is time-consuming, it can make the difference between a sale or no sale.

Detailed costs and time for checks 31 to 33

Around 5 minutes per product to take world–class photographs but you will need the right equipment. Professional photographers will charge a few hundred dollars per hour or you could hire the equipment and do it yourself.

Around 1 to 3 hours to create an item description template in HTML. Agencies will charge between $1000 and $3000 to do this for you, or a freelancer will charge $100 to $300 per hour.

10 to 30 minutes per listing to paste relevant product information into each.

Around 5 minutes per listing to carefully spellcheck.

Business impact

To gauge potential impact, measure if there's:

⊕ an increase in views (or clicks) to your listings

⊕ an increase in the number of items sold

⊕ an improvement in your conversion of visits to sales.

More information

See eBay's selling best practices tips at the Seller Centre:
http://goo.gl/cALV1R.

4

Establishing your brand

☑ CHECKS 34 TO 42
Make your brand consistent

What is it?

Wherever your eBay business name appears it must be consistent—for example, in email, user IDs, websites, business name, business cards, thank you slips and letterheads.

Three reasons to do it

Having a consistent brand means customers are more likely to remember you, return to you and tell others about you.

1 Consistency builds trust and attracts more *and* repeat customers.

2 A consistent brand can help you achieve higher prices and more sales.

3 Your brand will be transferable—to other marketplaces and websites, and offline.

Getting started

Once you've chosen a suitable name, update each of the following. If you have an existing business, make sure every one of these is consistent. *Make sure your business name is available before updating any!*

 Check 34: Business name   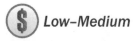 *Low–Medium*   *Low*

▮ Register your business name at ASIC: http://goo.gl/5so9T0.

Check 35: Business number *Low–Medium* *Low*

Create an Australian Business Number (ABN) at www.business.gov.au.

Check 36: Website address (S) *Low–Medium* *Low*

Register a website URL. Check with domain name providers by searching 'domain names' on Google.

Check 37: Email address (S) *Free–Low* *Low*

Create a new email with your provider (get free email addresses from Google, Microsoft and so on).

Check 38: Stationery

 Low–Medium *Medium–High*

Speak to a printer about bulk discounts for any stationery featuring your business name. Order new thank you slips, business cards, letterheads and other stationery.

Getting it done

Check 39: eBay User ID (S) *Free* *Low*

Update or register your eBay ID: <u>My eBay</u> > <u>Account</u> > <u>Account Information</u> > <u>Edit</u> (next to 'User ID').

Check 40: eBay store name  (S) *Low* *Low*

Update or register your eBay store name: <u>My eBay</u> > <u>Activity</u> > <u>Manage My Store</u> (in left navigation) > <u>Store Design</u> > <u>Change</u> (next to Display Settings).

Check 41: eBay email  Free Low

Update your registered eBay email address: <u>My eBay</u> > <u>Account</u> > <u>Account Information</u> > <u>Edit</u> (next to 'Registered email address').

Check 42: PayPal ID  Free Low

Update or register your PayPal ID. On PayPal: <u>My Account</u> > <u>Profile</u> > <u>Add or edit email</u> > <u>Add</u>.

Detailed costs and time for checks 34 to 42

⑨ ⊕ $200 and less than 1 hour to register a business name and Australian Business Number (ABN).

⑨ ⊕ $200 and less than 1 hour to register a website URL.

⑨ ⊕ $500 and up to a few days to design a new logo (search online).

⑨ ⊕ Cost will vary and a few weeks to update business stationery (search online).

Business impact

To gauge potential impact, measure if there's:

⊕ an increase in sales price

⊕ an increase in views (or clicks) to your listings

⊕ an increase in visits to your eBay store

⊕ an improvement in the feedback and DSR ratings you receive

⊖ a decrease in the number of questions buyers ask.

More information

Visit the Australian government website at http://goo.gl/LLkdo5 for when and how to register a business.

✓ CHECKS 43 TO 47
Have your store and listings professionally designed

What is it?

Individual branding is essential to stand out from other stores. You can use eBay store templates and create your own professional listings (see checks 31 to 33), or you can stand out from the crowd and invest in your business by paying a professional company to redesign both your store and listing template to help establish your brand.

Three reasons to do it

1 Professionally designed templates help build confidence in prospective buyers, which converts more visitors to buyers.

2 Professionally designed templates also project a more professional brand to encourage higher selling prices of your items and multiple purchases from each buyer.

3 It's important to stand out from your competitors by utilising a cutting-edge, unique and memorable design.

Getting started

Check 43: Mock up your design

($) *Free*   (🕐) *Low–Medium*

Choose a style and colours that best reflect your products and the personality of your business. Mock up a layout using basic design (pen and paper will do) but be clear on what you want your templates to look like.

Check 44: Get design quotes (💲) *Free* (🕐) *Low–Medium*

Contact three providers to get quotes on store and template redesign. Try Frooition (www.frooition.com/au), Dzine (www .dzine-hub.com) and a Google search for 'eBay store design'.

Check 45: Hire a designer

(💲) *Medium–High* (🕐) *Medium*

Employ your favourite designer/agency and agree on costs and timing.

Getting it done

You can ask your agency to update your store and listings as part of their quoted price, or you can do it yourself by completing these checks.

Check 46: Update your store template

(💲) *Free* (🕐) *Low–Medium*

Update this within My eBay > Activity > Manage My Store (in left navigation) > Store Design > Change (next to 'Display Settings').

Check 47: Update your listing template

(💲) *Free* (🕐) *High*

This is a more complicated process and will take some time. The process will vary depending on the listing tool you use. You will need to download all of your product information then slot this into the basic template for every item you sell.

> To add HTML (this is the language used for professionally designed templates) to an item description: <u>Sell</u> > <u>Sell an Item</u> > (beneath 'Add a description' in the Sell Your Item form) <u>HTML</u> > paste your code.

Detailed costs and time for checks 43 to 47

($) $1000 to $3000 and up to a few days to decide on a provider and submit your brief.

(⏰) Less than 1 hour and free to upload your new store design.

(⏰) Less than 5 hours and free to update your listing template.

Business impact

To gauge potential impact, measure if there's:

(+) an increase in your average sales price

(+) an increase in conversion of views to sales

(+) an increase in the number of items per buyer

(+) an increase in the number of repeat buyers.

More information

Visit eBay's Seller Centre at http://goo.gl/ronqW for more information on eBay Stores.

✓ CHECKS 48 TO 50
Create great product images

What is it?

In more than 15 years of eBay's existence one adage remains unchanged: 'a picture tells a thousand words', or to be more precise, pictures sell! Photographs are arguably the first and most important thing a prospective buyer looks at when deciding whether to click through to your listings or purchase from you. As competition in eCommerce increases, buyers have raised expectations for what they consider acceptable and appealing product photography. Remember that more clicks to your listing can help improve your visibility in eBay search results, so attract as many buyers as possible via the power of clear, crisp and attention-grabbing photography.

Three reasons to do it

At a time when the number of online businesses is greater than ever, all of them competing for buyer attention, this really is a non-negotiable.

1 Attract more buyers to your listing, which can help improve your standing in eBay's search results.

2 Convert more searchers to purchasers, resulting in more sales for your business.

3 *Not* doing it will diminish your ability to compete successfully in your category.

Getting started

Taking great photographs is often about having the right equipment to do so. If you plan on listing a lot of products on eBay it may be most cost-effective to purchase the equipment outright. Alternatively, you could consider hiring equipment whenever you need to create more photographs of your products. Some suppliers will allow you access to their stock photographs, but it's important to ensure they are the right size and as professional as possible.

Tip: Never copy and paste product images from the internet — you may be infringing copyright, which is against the law. From an eBay perspective, this could lead to your entire listing being ended and an inability to sell your stock. The risk is simply not worth it.

Check 48: Prepare products for photography

($) *Free* (clock) *Low–Medium*

Before you start taking photographs, prepare a sample of each product. This will save you time when you should be concentrating on completing the task at hand.

Getting it done

Before you begin, make sure you have a list of all of the products you're taking photos of, and the order in which you'll take them — this will make it easier for you to locate the right photographs later. Alternatively, you could save each image as you take it and rename it to the product name or number. Make sure each file is saved with a name that makes it fast and easy to identify and distinguish from other products.

Check 49: Photograph your products

 Free–Medium  Medium–High

Taking a great image is an art but there are some tips for making the end result look more professional.

- Use natural light wherever possible. For darker areas try to use lamps rather than the camera flash.

- Create a plain background. White often works best—a clean sheet is a simple option.

- Elevate products. Use a white stand or table; for clothing use a mannequin.

- Use a camera tripod to reduce shakes and bumps.

- Move the camera closer to the product rather than using zoom.

- Take images from a number of different angles.

Check 50: Upload your photos

Free High

Uploading images to eBay is a straightforward process once you have the image files saved to computer. However, there is no fast way to upload bulk images and assign them to individual listings unless you're using a third-party listing tool. To add a photo to your listing click Sell to enter the Sell Your Item form then Add Photos then Browse to locate your photo on your computer. Click the image then Open. Use the buttons to the right to optimise the image (crop, rotate, correct exposure, adjust brightness) and once you're happy with the image, click Upload.

Detailed costs and time for checks 48 to 50

- ⓢ A few hundred dollars to hire good photography equipment or up to a few thousand dollars to purchase it.
- ⓢ $200 to $500 per hour for a professional photographer.
- ⏱ 5 to 10 minutes per product to take the image.
- ⏱ 1 to 5 minutes per listing to upload to eBay.

Business impact

To gauge potential impact, measure if there's:

- ⊕ an increase in views (or clicks) to your listings
- ⊕ an increase in the number of items sold
- ⊖ a decrease in the number of questions asked by buyers.

More information

- View eBay's great photo tips page and video at http://goo.gl/k6ZeTu.

- You could consider investing in 360 product photography, which essentially takes a 360-degree image of your product (from all angles). Conduct a Google search for more information and equipment for sale.

5

Providing outstanding service

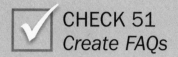

CHECK 51
Create FAQs

What is it?

FAQs provide buyers with answers to Frequently Asked Questions *before* they try to contact you. The more buyers who contact you, the more time you are forced to spend responding to them, and this is a cost centre for your business. Reducing contacts from customers reduces costs and therefore increases profits.

On eBay, if you have created FAQs a buyer who clicks to contact you will be routed via these automatically.

Three reasons to do it

1 Pre-empt your buyers' needs, providing outstanding service by pre-answering anticipated questions.

2 Reduce contacts from buyers, freeing up more time for you to invest in other areas of your business.

3 Ensure your service standards are consistent by providing standard written communications, which help make your business look more professional.

Getting started

Before you begin, you need to have a clear set of policies and information resources around various components of your eBay business. These can also form part of your overall business plan (as covered in check 12). FAQs will generally be required for areas such as:

- postage and handling
- payments
- returns

- general product information
- your contact details
- other business information.

Getting it done

Now you're ready to create FAQs for your buyers:

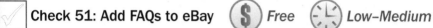

Check 51: Add FAQs to eBay *Free* *Low–Medium*

Click <u>My eBay</u> then <u>Account</u> then <u>Manage communications with buyers</u> then next to the heading 'Manage questions and answers' click <u>Edit</u> (or <u>Create</u>). On the next page, click the most relevant topic and click <u>Add more questions</u> to add additional FAQs. Once you have created all of your FAQs click <u>Submit</u>.

Detailed costs and time for check 51

- 30 to 60 minutes to create FAQs (depending on how many, and how detailed each is).
- Free to create and upload.

Business impact

To gauge potential impact, measure if there's:

- ⊖ a decrease in the number of questions buyers ask
- ⊖ a decrease in time spent on responding to buyer questions
- ⊕ an improvement in ratings left by buyers.

More information

For more about answering buyers' questions see the eBay page at http://goo.gl/2cJzxy.

✓ CHECKS 52 TO 55
Expand your service offering

What is it?

Providing great service also means providing various service options so you can appeal to as many buyers as possible. Expanding your service offering means you should provide multiple payment, postage, returns and contact options. Some things to consider:

- *Payments:* Offer PayPal as well as other services such as Paymate, credit card or bank deposit.

- *Postage:* Offer a short handling window of less than one day and consider offering fast, free alternatives. For more expensive items you may consider offering insurance, registered or courier services.

- *Returns:* Expand your returns window to longer than 30 days. eCommerce standards are gradually moving towards longer returns windows—in some cases, world-class service offers more than 180 days.

- *Contacts:* Offer a range of methods for buyers to contact you, including email, telephone or live chat.

Three reasons to do it

Offering more types of services gives your buyers more choice and helps you retain a competitive edge over other sellers on eBay.

1 Attract as many buyers as possible to your listings by providing additional services for those who have particular requirements.

2 Offering selected services may mean you qualify to receive the eBay Premium Service badge on your listings, which can attract more buyers.

3 By offering additional services, even if buyers do not utilise them, the overall impression is that your business is more professional. This can build more trust in your buyers and result in more sales.

Getting started

Expanding your service offerings is about pre-empting the needs of as many potential buyers as possible. Having said that, for some categories of product, buyer requirements could be quite narrow. There is no need to offer every single type of service available if that's not what your buyers want. The simplest way to gauge the most applicable services is to experiment with a number of listings before applying services across your entire inventory. It's not recommended to emulate other sellers as you may miss something buyers truly want. Simply copying another sellers' service offerings may mean both of you are less than optimal.

Getting it done

Most of your service offerings are uploaded to eBay via the Sell Your Item form. Click Sell at the top of any eBay page to access the form. Below is a list of suggested services for you to experiment with on selected listings before applying any to all of them. Test each one for a minimum of one month.

Check 52: Test payment options

 Free–Low **Low–Medium**

- *PayPal:* the most common form of payment used by eBay buyers. To open a PayPal account go to www.paypal.com.au.

- *Paymate:* similar to PayPal, and some buyers and sellers prefer to use it because it is an Australian company. To open a Paymate account go to www.paymate.com.

- *Credit card:* if your business has credit card processing capabilities it's a good idea to test whether your buyers would prefer to pay using this method, and via a number of different cards. Speak to your financial institution about card processing facilities or see more information about PayPal credit card processing at http://goo.gl/PQpf6q.

- *Bank deposit:* though tracking bank deposits can be time-consuming some customers still like to pay via this method.

Check 53: Test postage options

Free–Low **Low–Medium**

- standard postage
- expedited postage (such as Express Post)
- courier delivery
- registered post
- postage insurance

Check 54: Test returns options

- a returns period of less than 14 days
- a returns period of 30 days
- a returns period of greater than 30 days
- buyer pays return postage costs
- you cover return postage costs

Check 55: Test 'Contact us' options

- email is the default and should always be offered
- live chat via a free provider such as Skype (www.skype.com)
- telephone

At the end of your test period, highlight those service offerings that you will apply to all of your listings then bulk update your listing inventory using the process in check 11.

Detailed costs and time for checks 52 to 55

⑤ It costs nothing to offer additional services on your listings, though each service may cost you or your buyer a different or varying fee.

⏱ About 1 to 3 minutes per listing if updated individually or less if you update using eBay's bulk edit tool.

Business impact

To gauge potential impact, measure if there's:

(+) an increase in views (or clicks) to your listings

(+) an increase in the number of items sold, particularly on those listings that offer a complete range of services

(−) a reduction in complaints from buyers—expedited shipping, for example, may mean fewer buyers are disappointed by the time taken to receive their products.

More information

■ To find out more about eBay Premium Service visit http://goo.gl/rTkBen.

■ See eBay selling best practices tips at http://goo.gl/hwKatq.

✓ CHECK 56
Reduce your handling time

What is it?

In today's eCommerce world of increased expectations, buyers want to receive their products as quickly as possible. To keep up with buyer demand, you should ensure that you dispatch your products every day of the week, and keep your handling time to no more than 24 hours. On eBay, this is known as *same business day handling time*.

Three reasons to do it

To be competitive on eBay you need to offer world-class service levels. Reducing your handling time is one component of making your business as efficient as it can be.

1 Buyers want their products dispatched as quickly as possible. Having a same business day handling time may attract more clicks to your listings and more sales.

2 Offering a faster handling time means your listings may qualify for eBay's Fast & Free logo (where you offer free shipping) or Premium Service logo (where you offer free shipping, an express shipping method and 30-day money-back returns), both of which attract more buyer attention.

3 Fast product turnaround means a more efficient warehouse with less space used for storing products longer than you need to.

Getting started

Before you think about changing your handling time, make sure you choose a realistic period. Your handling time is used by eBay to help estimate dates for product delivery and sets expectations for your buyers. If you're unable to dispatch your products within each business day then do not make that promise to your buyers. Also remember that your handling time policy applies to *every* day of the week, so make sure you can deliver on that promise.

Getting it done

Buyers love fast delivery that includes a reduced handling time. Wherever possible, aim for same business day handling time.

Check 56: Update handling time

$ Free–Low   Low–Medium

You can update the handling time on all your listings at once by using the eBay bulk editing tool available when you subscribe to Selling Manager. Once subscribed, click My eBay then under the 'Selling Manager' heading click Active then check the box next to each listing you would like to edit before clicking Edit. On the bulk edit screen check the box next to the listings you wish to edit (or check the box at the top of the listings to edit all) then from the drop-down next to 'Edit' choose Handling time. Next to 'Handling time', choose 'Change to' from the drop-down arrows then choose your preferred time period. Click Save and close.

Detailed costs and time for check 56

⏱ Less than 5 minutes and free to update all of your listings at once if you use eBay's bulk listing editing tool.

Ⓢ $9.95 per month to subscribe to Selling Manager Pro (free if you subscribe to an eBay store).

Business impact

To gauge potential impact, measure if there's:

⊕ an increase in views (or clicks) to your listings

⊕ a faster average time taken for your buyers to receive their items

⊕ an improvement in the ratings left by your buyers.

More information

■ For more information on Fast & Free visit http://goo.gl/LQnNM1.

■ To see more about eBay Premium Service visit http://goo.gl/rTkBen.

■ To subscribe to Selling Manager or for more information visit http://goo.gl/4o26fL.

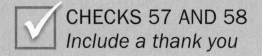

CHECKS 57 AND 58
Include a thank you

What is it?

You may think it is slightly quaint or outdated, but including a thank you with each shipment is the equivalent of retail store staff extending a friendly and appreciative farewell to customers to encourage them to return to buy again. On eBay, a thank you note can be just that, or it can include an offer of discounts on future purchases, a surprise free gift or more information about your eBay business and the products you sell. You can also remind your customers that you would love to hear from them via eBay's feedback and detailed seller rating systems.

Three reasons to do it

Not many eBay sellers utilise this tactic as a way to stand apart from their competitors, yet it is one of the most cost-effective ways to encourage more buyers to choose you over your competitors.

1 Create a more professional brand for your business (make sure you use quality design, printing and messaging).

2 Encourage more buyers to return to your eBay listings to purchase from you again.

3 Creating an overwhelmingly positive experience can lead to positive word of mouth and an increase in free traffic to your eBay listings.

Getting started

It's a good idea to trial a few different types of thank you notes for your eBay customers. You need to be able to measure, as much as possible, the results that each type of thank you delivers for your business. It's advisable to design your own to begin with to see which types work best, then consider having them professionally created. The more professional your thank you looks, the better impact it is likely to have on your buyers.

Check 57: Test thank you options

($) *Free–Medium*   (🕐) *Low–Medium*

Create a marketing plan using a variety of thank you notes. Test each of the following for one to two weeks:

- *A plain thank you*—a simple message on a card to thank customers for their business. Include your store's URL.

- *A more detailed thank you*—a message to thank buyers for their business. Include a note about your returns policy, details for how to contact you and a polite request for them to leave positive buyer comments and ratings.

- *A thank you gift*—something simple and inexpensive that nonetheless reflects your brand. Remember to be professional and make sure the gift is received in perfect condition.

- *An incentive thank you*—encouraging the buyer to buy from you again. The easiest way to do this is to offer a percentage refund via PayPal. Ask buyers to email you when they purchase again and send them the refund amount immediately.

Tip: Store subscribers can print promotional flyers to showcase their current product range. Go to <u>My eBay</u> click <u>Account</u> then <u>Manage My Store</u> then <u>Promotional Flyer</u>.

Getting it done

Now you have tested which type of thank you resonates the most with your buyers, as measured by your buyer ratings and comments, and the percentage of buyers who are repeat customers.

Check 58: Include a thank you

($) Free–Low **(⏰) Low–Medium**

Include your best-performing thank you in every package you send to all but 10 per cent of customers, who become your control group to test whether your thank you is continuing to make a difference. You should make a note of the buyer IDs of those who receive no thank you, then look at their feedback comments and the percentage of those who return to you.

You can quickly see the percentage of your total buyers who are repeat customers by going to My eBay then click Account then click Sales Reports and look for the number next to the heading 'Repeat buyers %'.

Detailed costs and time for checks 57 and 58

⏰ 1 month to test which type of thank you receives the best response.

⏰ Less than 1 minute to include the thank you in each package you send.

⏰ 1 to 3 hours per month to measure the impact of the thank you.

($) Costs vary depending on the form of thank you. Basic thank you notes will cost only the paper and printing. Small gifts should cost less than $5, depending on your product sold price. Percentage refunds should be about ten per cent, but test as high as 20 per cent.

Business impact

To gauge potential impact, measure if there's:

⊕ an increase in the number of repeat buyers

⊕ an increase in the number of visits to your eBay store

⊕ an improvement to the ratings left by your buyers

⊖ a decrease in the number of negative ratings left by buyers.

More information

A nice little blog on 25 ways to thank your customers can be found at http://goo.gl/Ivf0uA.

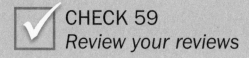

CHECK 59
Review your reviews

What is it?

On eBay, some buyers choose to leave you feedback ratings and comments, and detailed seller ratings on certain aspects of your service such as postage time, communications and postage costs. Your performance in these areas is compared with that of other sellers and outstanding service can lead to improved visibility in search results. Buyers often compare seller ratings and this can be decisive in whether or not they buy from you. When you get caught up in running a business, it's often easy to overlook these ratings or forget to monitor your performance over time. Reviewing your reviews is a great way to hear directly from your customers and make changes to any of your business operations that are leading to customer dissatisfaction.

Three reasons to do it

Most businesses pay a lot of money to survey their customers for their views on service levels and other areas of performance. On eBay, the feedback and detailed ratings systems are in-built, so you have the potential to get to hear from your customers directly every time you make a sale.

1 Solve minor problems before they become larger ones.

2 Ensure you are competitive with other sellers in your category to help optimise your visibility in eBay search results.

3 Every business should be listening to their customers' feedback—the good, the bad and the indifferent. Hearing your customers' views will help you refine your service offerings and may lead to increased sales.

Getting started

Monitoring your performance is a critical component of ongoing commercial success. An alert business owner is faster to respond to issues before they become major problems. Reviewing your reviews can also form part of a successful business plan, as outlined in check 12. The reviews you should be reviewing at least monthly are:

- *overall feedback rating:* view within <u>My eBay</u> then click the number after your user ID

- *individual feedback comments:* view within <u>My eBay</u> then click the number after your user ID

- *detailed seller ratings:* view within <u>My eBay</u> then click the number after your user ID

- *email comments received by buyers:* create two feedback folders within My Messages, one for positive and one for negative feedback. Click <u>My eBay</u> then <u>Messages</u> then under the heading 'Folders' click <u>Add a folder</u>. Enter the folder name then click <u>Save</u>.

Getting it done

Make a diary reminder to review your reviews each month.

Check 59: Create a review spreadsheet

 Free **Low–Medium**

Create a spreadsheet with the following column headings:

- Month

- Number of positive feedback comments received (% of total comments)

- Keywords from positive comments (scan your positive comments for commonly recurring keywords and enter them into this field)

- Number of negative feedback comments received
- Keywords from negative comments (scan your negative comments for commonly recurring keywords and enter them into this field)
- Item as described rating
- Communication rating
- Postage time rating
- Postage and handling charges rating
- Positive email comments (scan your positive feedback message folder for commonly recurring keywords and enter them into this field)
- Negative email comments (scan your positive feedback message folder for commonly recurring keywords and enter them into this field)
- Other feedback (given via the phone, mail or in person, for example).

Now, compare each month's performance versus the last. Look for significant changes in trend. Finally, in the last column (label it Action), make a note of changes you need to make to your business in order to enhance positive comments or reduce negative ones.

Tip: You can find software online to help you scan comments to find common keywords. Conduct a Google search for 'wordles'.

Detailed costs and time for check 59

⏱ 3 to 5 hours each month to complete your spreadsheet and create an action plan for improvement.

⑤ Reviewing your customer comments is free.

Business impact

To gauge potential impact, measure if there's:

(+) an increase in your overall positive ratings

(+) an increase in views to your listings that convert to sales.

More information

To find out about feedback on eBay go to http://goo.gl/TfGqRc.

6

Mastering logistics

✓ CHECKS 60 AND 61
Reorganise your warehouse

What is it?

Whether you operate your eBay business from home, an existing business or a warehouse, it's critical that you or your staff can locate any given product as quickly as possible. The longer it takes you to find a product, the more you pay in resources. Consider a business that sells 30 000 products each year. In a poorly organised warehouse, it could take an average of 30 wasted seconds to find each product for dispatch. Over one year that equates to 250 hours of pointless labour and even at $15 per hour that's $3750 wasted salary. Whatever the scale or location of your business, the principle is the same: wasted time is lost profit.

Three reasons to do it

Greater efficiency equals more profit; it's as simple as that.

1 Less wasted time equals higher profit margins.

2 Faster location of products means faster receipt by buyers, leading to happier customers and more chance of repeat business.

3 A well-organised warehouse can mean reducing time spent stocktaking and increasing ability to gauge when products may be about to run out of stock or to identify loss through damage or theft.

Getting started

Successful warehousing is all about careful planning.

Check 60: Create a warehouse map

($) Free–Low   **Low–Medium**

The key to successful organisation is to create a map of your warehouse or storage space and label each section where product is to be kept. You will need both a map of the area and a spreadsheet for which product is to be placed in each section. Aim for uniformity—Aisle, Section, Shelf and so on. Your map should be saved in a safe place and created in a format that allows for easy reorganisation or expansion.

Once the map is complete, you then need to decide how your products are going to be allocated. Decide on a system that works best for you and is easy to follow. This could depend on:

- alphabetisation
- product code—number order
- product size
- supplier group
- manual numbering.

Each time you receive stock make a note of where it is placed in your warehouse.

Getting it done

Armed with your complete storage or warehouse layout, your map should now clearly show where every product is to be kept. Now you can create a note for each product on eBay detailing where in the warehouse it is kept. This note is not seen by buyers and can be printed for each order, making it much faster for you or your staff to locate products—which means your buyers will also receive them faster.

Check 61: Add product location notes

 Free–Low **Medium–High**

Use the eBay bulk listing editing tool to add a location note to each product. You need to subscribe to Selling Manager to use the bulk editing tool. Once subscribed, click My eBay then under the 'Selling Manager' heading click Active. Check the Edit box at the top of the page to highlight all listings then click Edit. On the bulk edit screen, click Customise on the right then click Custom label and click the arrow pointing to the right then click Apply changes. The custom label column will now appear on the screen. Double-click the field next to each listing to enter the warehouse location of the product. Click Submit all.

Detailed costs and time for checks 60 and 61

🕐 1 to several hours to create a map of your warehouse plus product locations, depending on size.

🕐 Less than 1 minute per listing to add a customer label on eBay for location.

$ Creating a map of your warehouse and adding a custom label on eBay are cost free.

Business impact

To gauge potential impact, measure if there's:

⊕ an increase in your productivity (or that of your staff). Record and keep track of how many products are being picked per hour

⊖ a decrease in instances of running out of stock of products

⊕ an improvement to your and your team's morale. Though this is hard to measure, a tidy and clean workplace is not only healthier and safer, it can lead to happier and more productive staff.

More information

Conduct a Google search for 'effective warehouse layout' to see examples and businesses that can assist with this process.

CHECKS 62 TO 65
Source multiple service providers

What is it?

As your business grows, one postal/courier service provider may not be able to provide you with the most competitively priced logistics solution. Different providers may be more competitive on specific service offerings so it's best to employ a range of suppliers to ensure you, and your buyers, always receive the best possible deal.

Three reasons to do it

1 Investing time in getting a wide variety of quotes may result in lower delivery fees for your business.

2 Lowering your delivery charges may enable you to offer free shipping for all your products, giving you a competitive edge.

3 Having more than one provider means you'll have leverage to negotiate, and fall-back options should one provider fail to meet your expectations.

Getting started

Check 62: Create a product specifications spreadsheet

($) *Free* (⏱) *Low–Medium*

Create a spreadsheet of your product types, volumes and dimensions, as well as a sample of customer locations.

Check 63: Create a shortlist of providers

($) *Free* (clock) *Low–Medium*

Conduct online research to make a shortlist of eight to ten delivery providers who look best able to suit your business's needs. Consider a comparison site such as Temando (www.temando.com).

Check 64: Negotiate great quotes

($) *Free* (clock) *Medium–High*

Speak to a sales representative at each of your shortlisted companies. Avoid accepting publicly available quotes—your job is to sell the potential of your business as being an important customer, and to negotiate the best possible rates.

Getting it done

Check 65: Integrate service providers

($) *Free–Low* (clock) *Medium–High*

Decide on your final list of providers after you have received all quotes, and integrate these into your eBay listings. To update all of your listings simultaneously using Selling Manager Pro: My eBay > Inventory > Active > check the box at the top of your listings > use the Edit drop-down to edit all > within the edit listings screen check the box at the top of your listings, use the Edit drop-down for 'Postage domestic' > under 'Services' select your new service > enter Cost > enter Discount > Save and close > Submit all.

Detailed costs and time for checks 62 to 65

⊛ ⑤ Free and a few hours to create a spreadsheet of your logistics requirements (see below).

⊛ ⑤ Free and a few hours to dedicate some time to exploring a range of service providers.

Business impact

To gauge potential impact, measure if there's:

⊖ a decrease in your average postage paid

⊖ a decrease in your buyer's average postage paid

⊕ an increase in your number of sold items

⊕ an improvement in the postage-related ratings left by your buyers.

More information

Visit Temando at http://goo.gl/wPPSId for more information on integrating a complete solutions provider.

CHECK 66
Sign up to Click and Send

What is it?

Click and Send is an Australia Post service that allows you to pay for and print postage labels, attach them to eBay-branded satchels and place them in a post box...without having to visit an Australia Post counter. Even better, each parcel is tracked, meaning more certainty for buyers and less likelihood of your products being lost.

Three reasons to do it

Click and Send can save you precious time and money and help you be more effective at measuring your postage costs.

1 Pay less for professional-looking, eBay-branded satchels and boxes, which means more profit for you, and a better brand image than using non-branded packaging.

2 Save time (and therefore boost profits) by placing your packages directly into Australia Post boxes without the need for lining up to pay for postage.

3 All Click and Send packages receive a tracking number, meaning your buyers can trace their progress and get clear expectations on when they are likely to receive their products.

Getting started

Before signing up, read all the relevant information on the Australia Post website at http://goo.gl/m49Ehq. In particular, make sure you are aware of the terms and conditions for using the service, and associated costs.

Getting it done

Signing up for Click and Send is a simple process of a few steps.

☑ **Check 66: Register for Click and Send** 💲 *Free* 🕐 *Low*

> On the Australia Post website (see p. 101) click the <u>Register now</u> button then click <u>Register for Click and Send</u> beneath the red <u>Login</u> button. Complete the registration form then click <u>Submit</u>. Complete registration by clicking the <u>Link with eBay</u> button—this will link your eBay sales with the Click and Send functionality. You will also need to check your email inbox to confirm your registration.
>
> *Tip:* Look out for Postage Labels new to eBay, which give you the ability to print your own postage labels to attach to your eBay packages. Find more information at http://goo.gl/rcY3FV.

Detailed costs and time for check 66

- ⊕ 💲 Around 10 minutes and free to register for Click and Send.
- 💲 Costs for postal products vary—see the Australia Post website for more information.

Business impact

To gauge potential impact, measure if there's:

- ⊖ a decrease in costs paid on packaging such as satchels and boxes
- ⊖ a decrease in time spent on paying for postage
- ⊕ an improvement in postage-related ratings left by buyers
- ⊖ a reduction in non-received item claims from your buyers.

More information

For an overview of the Click and Send service visit the Australia Post website at http://goo.gl/EvvmKD.

✓ CHECKS 67 TO 69
Improve your packaging

What is it?

I've heard stories of some eBay sellers wrapping their products in a garbage bag and sending it to buyers. While this example may be an urban legend, it does highlight a genuine opportunity for eBay businesses to continue to delight their buyers throughout the buying experience. Secure packaging that ensures your products arrive safely is non-negotiable, but you may also want to consider the impression that branded packaging makes. Other sellers secure their package but use so much tape that it takes buyers way too long to open it, and they may cause damage to the product in doing so. Striking the right balance with packaging that looks great and products that are secure but accessible is the ideal to aim for.

You may also wish to consider the actual packaging your product comes in. This is a different concept from how you choose to wrap it before sending. Think about your packaging as summing up your complete brand experience — what does it say about your business?

Tip: You can ask your supplier(s) if they can repackage their products specifically for resale on eBay. For some of them, the chance to slightly rebrand for the eBay marketplace might help solve potential channel conflicts.

Three reasons to do it

Great packaging can mean the difference between an acceptable buyer experience and one that far exceeds buyer expectations.

1 The right packaging can better protect your products, meaning fewer buyer complaints and returns, which all adds up to more profit for you.

2 Branded packaging can help boost your reputation as a seller—packaging that delights customers leads to repeat purchases and strong word of mouth.

3 eBay sellers who invest significantly in their overall experience with superior packaging are still in the minority, so doing so will give you a strong competitive advantage.

Getting started

When opting to work with a supplier, it's always important to choose one that is both price competitive and well aligned with your business objectives.

Check 67: Find an agency   ($) *Free*   *Medium*

> Conduct an internet search to find three agencies that will be able to design your packaging. This could also include a logistics company who can provide unbranded but high-quality packaging. Write a brief document about what you want and need, including the type and quantity of products you sell, where you post them and any fragile items you post. Compare quotes and service levels of each before deciding which is best for your business. Remember to include the cost of packaging in your profit and loss spreadsheet, as outlined in check 13.

Check 68: Agree on a design

($) *Medium–High*   *Medium*

> After you have chosen your preferred provider, you need to carefully agree on the design of your packaging. Your provider should be integrated into your business to the extent that they have a hands-on approach with your products, understand your

business goals and appreciate your logistics challenges. There is no point paying for a beautiful design that is impractical. For this reason, it's advisable to avoid using an offshore company.

Getting it done

Once you have received your professionally branded packaging, you need to measure its performance.

Check 69: Track performance   ($) *Free*   (⏰) *Medium*

Create a simple spreadsheet to help you keep track of your packaging's performance. You should know exactly how many products are damaged in transit each month with a brief comment on the circumstances around the damage. Keep track of any specific customer comments. You can then feed this back to your provider so they can make tweaks to the packaging for future production. Remember to update any product information on the packaging if your buyers frequently ask about the same issue.

Detailed costs and time for checks 67 to 69

- About one month to find the right provider for your packaging.

- 1 to 2 months to brief the provider properly and have them supply you with mock-ups for the packaging.

- 1 to 2 months for the packaging to be printed and delivered.

- Costs will vary depending on your requirements and the size of your order. Try to keep costs per unit to a minimum—they should never exceed about ten per cent of the sale price of the product and must remain within your profit margin.

Business impact

To gauge potential impact, measure if there's:

- ⊕ an improvement in ratings left by your buyers
- ⊕ more repeat customers
- ⊖ a reduction in products damaged in transit.

More information

A fantastic inspirational site can be found at http://goo.gl/q4NeAZ.

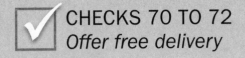

CHECKS 70 TO 72
Offer free delivery

What is it?

As business owners, we all know there is no such thing as 'free' delivery. However, buyers tend to respond very positively to the word *free*. In the eCommerce example, 'free' means the buyer can be assured of no nasty surprise costs associated with receiving their product. Most buyers understand that the cost is incorporated into the item price, but feel reassured that they are paying only the actual cost of postage and sellers do not tack on an additional cost once the transaction has begun. Free delivery has become more common than paid-for delivery on eBay so offering it to your customers means you will remain competitive. Of course, for some products and categories offering free delivery is not possible, so always check the most popular sellers in your category and ensure your postage costs are at least comparable.

You may also wish to offer additional postal services such as expedited shipping, insurance, registered post or courier delivery. Most buyers accept that these services attract an additional cost.

Tip: If you cannot afford to offer free delivery you may wish to consider offering postage discounts for multiple purchases. For more information visit http://goo.gl/q2B2SI.

Three reasons to do it

More buyers are demanding free delivery as an eCommerce standard. Free delivery is one component of having the eBay Premium Service badge appear on your listings, helping you stand out from other sellers in your category.

1 Most eCommerce leaders do—if you don't you may not be competitive.

2 The power of 'free' can increase sales.

3 Often free delivery results in fewer buyer complaints. Buyers hate seeing delivery costs lower than they have paid—it's a risky profiteering strategy that rarely pays off.

Getting started

First, you need to experiment to gauge which shipping strategy is best for you and your products.

Check 70: Test shipping options

 **Free–Medium** **Medium–High**

Experiment with each of the following free shipping strategies:

- actual product price + actual delivery fee
- reduced product price + increased delivery fee
- increased product price + free delivery.

You can do this either by creating three identical listings aside from the shipping details, or by running each strategy for a minimum of two weeks. Remember that the most successful strategy will vary by product type and depend on what your competitors are doing.

Getting it done

Now you have worked out your best shipping strategy, it's time to implement it and measure the results.

Check 71: Update shipping options

 ($) Free–Low **(clock) Medium–High**

You can quickly update your shipping and product prices using eBay's bulk listing editing tool, available to Selling Manager Pro subscribers. In <u>My eBay</u> under the 'Selling Manager' heading click <u>Active</u> then check the box next to each listing you wish to edit then click <u>Edit</u>. On the bulk edit page check the box of all listings to receive the same postage rate then click <u>Postage (Domestic)</u>. Specify your postage costs and change the product price (if applicable). It will take more time to also replace the relevant information within your item description. You can do this on the bulk edit screen by clicking <u>Item Description</u> and using the find and replace functionality. Once complete, click <u>Submit all.</u>

Check 72: Measure postage performance

($) Free **(clock) Medium**

As part of your profit and loss spreadsheet it's critical always to assess how much postage you are paying to ensure it is safely within a healthy profit margin. Your postage strategy is not 'set and forget', so it would be wise to group your eBay listings into like-postage to compare relative sales.

Detailed costs and time for checks 70 to 72

($) $9.95 per month to subscribe to Selling Manager Pro (free if you subscribe to an eBay store).

(clock) 1 to 6 weeks to conduct your pricing strategy tests.

(clock) Less than 1 minute per listing to update your pricing if you use eBay's bulk listing editing tool.

Business impact

To gauge potential impact, measure if there's:

⊕ an increase in views (or clicks) to your listings

⊕ an increase in the number of items sold

⊕ an improvement in postage-related ratings (note that those products sold with free delivery automatically receive a detailed seller rating of 5 out of 5).

More information

- A recent US report highlights some of the key benefits and concerns of offering free shipping at http://goo.gl/BBP1HI.

- For more about eBay Premium Service visit http://goo.gl/rTkBen.

- To subscribe to Selling Manager and for more information visit http://goo.gl/4o26fL.

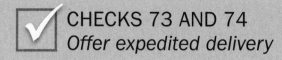

CHECKS 73 AND 74
Offer expedited delivery

What is it?

Fast is becoming the new norm in eCommerce. Some websites offer metropolitan customers the opportunity to receive their products within three hours. It is a sign of things to come: buyers will expect eCommerce delivery standards to offer the same level of instant gratification that shopping in a retail mall would deliver.

Three reasons to do it

As buyer expectations continue to raise the eCommerce service bar, sellers slow to adapt to these demands will be left behind. Offering an expedited delivery option is one component of having the eBay Premium Service badge appear on your listings, helping you stand out from other sellers in your category.

1 Some buyers want the certainty of expedited delivery and are prepared to pay extra for it. If you do not offer this as an option you may be losing these potential customers.

2 Expedited delivery options keep you competitive with the best eCommerce merchants around the world, but also with bricks-and-mortar retailers, giving your buyers that near-instant gratification they often crave.

3 Expedited delivery can in some instances lead to less buyer remorse, which may result in fewer product returns.

Getting started

Using the website of each of the various shipping providers, compile a list of expedited delivery options.

☑ Check 73: Research expedited delivery options

💲 *Free*   🕐 *Medium*

Your list of expedited delivery costs and time should be grouped by provider and product type. Larger and heavier products will generally cost more. Before choosing options, speak with each provider to ensure their services are available in your specific area and for your specific products.

Getting it done

Once you have compiled your list of expedited delivery options and their respective costs, it's time to update your eBay listings.

☑ Check 74: Update shipping options

💲 *Free-Low*   🕐 *Medium-High*

You can quickly add expedited delivery options using eBay's bulk listing editing tool, available to Selling Manager Pro subscribers. In <u>My eBay</u> under the 'Selling Manager' heading click <u>Active</u> then check the box next to each listing you wish to edit then click <u>Edit</u>. On the bulk edit page, check the box of all listings to receive expedited shipping then click <u>Postage (Domestic)</u>. Specify the service you're offering then click <u>Save and close</u>. It will take more time to also replace the relevant information within your item description. You can do this on the bulk edit screen by clicking <u>Item Description</u> and using the find and replace functionality. Once complete, click <u>Submit all</u>.

Detailed costs and time for checks 73 and 74

⑤ $9.95 per month to subscribe to Selling Manager Pro (free if you subscribe to an eBay store).

⏱ 3 to 5 hours to compile a list of expedited delivery providers.

⏱ Less than 1 minute to update each of your listings using eBay's bulk editing tool.

⑤ Costs for expedited delivery will vary but your buyers will generally pay for the additional services.

Business impact

To gauge potential impact, measure if there's:

⊕ an increase in views (or clicks) to your listings

⊕ an increase in the number of items sold (of up to 11 per cent, according to eBay—to see more go to http://goo.gl/lXtQk9)

⊖ a decrease in product returns.

More information

■ To find out more about eBay Premium Service visit http://goo.gl/rTkBen.

■ To subscribe to Selling Manager and for more information visit http://goo.gl/4o26fL.

✓ CHECK 75
Offer extended returns

What is it?

Another common eCommerce standard is to offer an extended window for buyers to return products if they are dissatisfied with their purchase. Contrary to popular belief, some sellers have found that there has been no increase in the percentage of orders returned but a noticeable increase in the number of items sold. World-class practices include 365-day returns; some even offer unlimited returns, though naturally conditions apply!

What can be more challenging is how you handle returns. Some businesses actively encourage you to purchase multiple products so you can try them out at home and simply return the ones you don't want. Other businesses cover postage both ways for the buyer to return their products (and receive replacements), while others offer money-back returns. The important thing to remember is to remain highly competitive within your category, and offering better policies than your competitors may give you that much-needed edge.

Three reasons to do it

Offering extended and favourable returns conditions increases buyer confidence and may result in more sales. Offering money-back returns of 30 days or more is one component of having the eBay Premium Service badge appear on your listings, helping you stand out from other sellers in your category.

1 Instil increased buyer confidence to convert more visits to your listings to sales.

2 Offer more favourable returns policies than other sellers in your category to gain a valuable competitive advantage.

3 A clear and generous returns policy can lead to fewer buyer complaints and negative ratings.

Getting started

Whatever your returns policy, there is always scope to extend it and gauge whether this attracts more buyers or more sales. Consider the following options:

- *Duration.* Fourteen days is the minimum you should reasonably offer, though 30 days is the minimum to qualify for eBay Premium Service. To be of world class, consider 100- or 365-day returns.

- *Costs.* Your options are for you to cover the cost of returning the product and sending a replacement, for you and the buyer to share these costs, or for the buyer to pay both.

- *Policy.* Your options are a replacement product, a similar product to the same value, or money back, which is required to qualify for eBay Premium Service.

- *Conditions.* These vary depending on the product type but may be for breakages, wrong sizes or change of mind, for example. You might also consider whether the package needs to be unopened and/or in its original packaging. Best in class is to offer returns with no conditions attached.

Getting it done

Once you have decided on your returns policies, you need to update your eBay listings.

☑ Check 75: Update your returns policy

$ Free–Low   **🕐 Low–Medium**

You can quickly update your returns policy using eBay's bulk listing editing tool, available to Selling Manager Pro subscribers. In <u>My eBay</u> under the 'Selling Manager' heading click <u>Active</u> then check the box next to each listing you wish to edit then click <u>Edit</u>. On the bulk edit page, check the box of all listings to receive expedited shipping then click <u>Returns policy</u>. Specify the service you're offering then click <u>Save and close</u>. Remember also to replace the relevant information within your item description. You can do this on the bulk edit screen by clicking <u>Item Description</u> and using the find and replace functionality. Once complete, click <u>Submit all</u>.

You can also create your returns policy using eBay's Business Policies functionality. For more information about this visit http://goo.gl/T3lue7.

Detailed costs and time for check 75

$ $9.95 per month to subscribe to Selling Manager Pro (free if you subscribe to an eBay store).

🕐 Less than 1 minute to update each listing if you use eBay's bulk editing tool.

Business impact

To gauge potential impact, measure if there's:

⊕ an increase in conversion of views or clicks to your listing to sales

⊖ a decrease in negative ratings left by buyers.

More information

- Note that the Australian Consumer and Competition Commission (ACCC) advises consumers they have the right to ask for repairs, replacements or refunds under certain circumstances at http://goo.gl/ONkNhv.

- To subscribe to Selling Manager and for more information visit http://goo.gl/4o26fL.

7

Marketing your products and your business

CHECK 76
Submit products to eBay Deals

What is it?

eBay Deals is a special area of the website where buyers come to find new products at unbeatable prices. In order to submit your products, you need to satisfy eBay's guidelines, which include the following:

- new products
- Buy It Now format
- sufficient quantities
- a Good Til Cancelled eBay store listing
- free postage.

A full list of criteria can be found at http://goo.gl/QT7Wyg.

Three reasons to do it

eBay carefully curates its deals database based on what buyers are looking for. Some buyers shop exclusively in the Deals area of the site so your participating can help tap into a whole new segment of customers.

1 Receive additional traffic to your listings and your eBay store.

2 While you may have to reduce the price of your products, high-profile events can result in a high volume of sales, meaning more profit for you.

3 Buyers subscribe to the Deals daily newsletter, which raises the profile of your business.

Getting started

You need to submit your best-performing products to eBay Deals, and those that you can offer the best discount on. Some sellers use deals as loss leaders (a retail term that means you are prepared to make no profit on the sale in the hope that it will motivate buyers to purchase other products with higher margins), but this is a risky strategy and you should always aim to make at least some profit. Participation in Deals is a great way to build brand awareness for your business. You will need to supply eBay with proof of the recommended retail price of each product you submit, so do this research first.

Getting it done

Applying to participate in Deals is an automated process.

Check 76: Apply to join Deals ($) Free (🕐) Low–Medium

Have all of the relevant information ready or the relevant listings open on your computer so you can quickly copy and paste the information. Submit your products at this page: http://goo.gl/HOsNAH.

Detailed costs and time for check 76

🕐 About five minutes per product.

($) It costs nothing to participate, aside from the discount you offer your buyers.

Business impact

To gauge potential impact, measure if there's:

⊕ an increase in views (or clicks) to your listings included in the Deals area of the site

⊕ an increase in the number of items sold as part of Deals

⊕ an increase in sales of non-Deals items as buyers click through to see your store and other listings.

More information

You can find out more about eBay Deals at http://goo.gl/MBUa0b.

✓ CHECKS 77 AND 78
Optimise for search engine keywords

What is it?

A common mistake eBay sellers make is to assume that once they have listed on the site, they do not need to invest any resources in driving more traffic to their listings. The simple fact is that you can never have too many potential buyers, so anything you can do to attract more is good for business. Within eBay Stores, there is a functionality to use Google and other search engines to drive customers directly to your eBay listings. There is no additional charge (aside from your monthly store subscription) to drive this traffic to your listings.

Three reasons to do it

Promoting your eBay store is your responsibility. Don't ever rely on buyers to find you—you need to help them by promoting your store in as many places as possible.

1   You can never have too many potential buyers, and it's a great way to bring customers from outside eBay to your eBay store.

2   It's fast and very easy to set up.

3   It costs no additional money for this potentially high-impact tool.

Getting started

Start by conducting some research to decide on the best search engine keywords for your products.

Check 77: Research top keywords

$ Free   **⏰ Low–Medium**

Use Google's keyword generator to help gauge the best-performing keywords for your products and categories: http://goo.gl/qmrzgP.

Getting it done

Creating your keyword list on eBay is a fast and simple process. It's advisable to review your list every few months to ensure you have optimally performing words.

Check 78: Update store keywords   **$ Free***   **⏰ Low**

In My eBay click <u>Account</u> then <u>Manage My Store</u> then <u>Search Engine Keywords</u> to create your list.

Detailed costs and time for checks 77 and 78

⏰ Less than 1 hour to create your search engine keyword list.

$ Store subscriptions range in price from $19.95 to $499.95 per month.

*Free to add search keywords once you subscribe to a store.

Business impact

To gauge potential impact, measure if there's:

(+) an increase in traffic to your eBay store

(+) an increase in traffic to your eBay store coming direct from Google (you can measure this via your store's reporting, available from within your store hub—click My eBay then Account then Manage My Store then Traffic Report).

More information

Watch the helpful video on Google Keyword Planner at http://goo.gl/p1LWSQ.

✓ CHECKS 79 TO 82
Cross-promote

What is it?

You can drive more potential customers to your eBay listings by cross-promoting your products in various parts of the site. eBay offers this service for free to eBay Stores subscribers and it's a great opportunity to have your products seen by more potential customers. Your listings will be displayed when a buyer conducts a relevant search or transaction.

Three reasons to do it

There are not many opportunities on eBay to drive sales during key moments of a buyer's transaction. Wherever possible, using eBay's automated promotional tools shows buyers highly relevant messages when they're in the process of deciding what to buy.

1 You can never have too many potential buyers and it's a great way to attract more customers to your listings.

2 It's fast and very easy to set up.

3 It costs no additional money for this potentially high-impact tool.

Getting started

Before you begin, you need to make sure you're promoting the best possible combination of products from your inventory.

Check 79: Add a page counter ($) Free (🕐) Low–Medium

Start by making sure you have a page view or visitor counter enabled on your listings. Knowing how many people view your items, compared with how many people buy them, is a good way of working out your conversion ratio, a measure of popularity. You can only add a counter during the listing process or by revising your listings one at a time. Simply click Revise item at the top of your 'View item' page.

Check 80: Create a popular product report

($) Free (🕐) Medium–High

Next, create a report of your most popular items. In My eBay click Active to view watchers for each live listing—this will give you an indication of your product's popularity. Also in My eBay click Account then Sales Report to download your sales history. This will tell you which products have sold the most. Finally, work out your view-to-sales ratio and watches-to-sales ratio. The higher the percentage, the more popular your item is.

Getting it done

Once you have worked out which of your items are most popular, sign up for eBay's cross-promotion tools. You need to subscribe to an eBay store to do this.

Check 81: Create cross-promotions

($) Free–Low (🕐) Medium

To access the cross-promotion tool, click My eBay then Account then Manage My Store. Under Item Promotion on the left click Cross-Promotion then Manage to establish your default and

Edit to change your settings. You can choose to show any of your store categories or specific keywords from your item titles. When editing your settings you can choose when to participate in cross-promotions and what kinds of listings to display.

Check 82: Refresh cross-promotions

($) *Free–Low* **(clock)** *Medium*

Make yourself a calendar reminder to refresh your cross-promotions at least every month. You need to ensure that your most popular products are always used in cross-promotions.

Detailed costs and time for checks 79 to 82

($) $19.95 to $499.95 per month to subscribe to an eBay store.

(clock) 1 to 2 hours to create your popular products report.

(clock) 10 to 20 minutes to activate your cross-promotion settings.

Business impact

To gauge potential impact, measure if there's:

(+) an increase in views (or clicks) to the listings you show within cross-promotions

(+) an overall increase in the number of items sold.

More information

Learn more about participating in cross-promotions at http://goo.gl/aMA8kY.

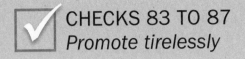

CHECKS 83 TO 87
Promote tirelessly

What is it?

You should never stop promoting your eBay business. Use every sensible opportunity to tell people about your eBay business and the kinds of products you sell. As the business owner, it is your responsibility to spread the word about your eBay business. Some sellers assume that paying the fees to eBay is all they need to do to attract as many buyers as possible. The most successful sellers, however, take charge of additional promotions. You can do this in a number of ways. Consider:

- promotional flyers
- letterbox drops
- online advertising
- offline advertising
- word of mouth.

Three reasons to do it

Professional and effective marketing can drive significantly more traffic to your eBay store. Remember that each store receives its own unique URL (or web address) so you can send customers directly to your eBay transactional site. Often, establishing an eBay store and promoting it can be more cost-effective than building your own website from scratch.

1 You can never have too many potential buyers and it's a great way to attract more customers to your store.

2 Professional marketing and advertising can improve your brand perception and help build buyer confidence.

3 If you make sure your marketing is directly measurable you will be able to continually optimise performance, driving more traffic to your store for less money.

Getting started

As with many components of operating a business, success begins with careful planning. In the case of promotion, you need to set yourself a clear budget, understand who your target customers are, create professional collateral and measure each campaign.

Check 83: Create a marketing plan

($) *Free*   **(🕐)** *Medium–High*

A successful marketing plan will include:

- types of marketing
- target audience demographics and size
- expected response rate (how many buyers receiving the promotion will act upon it)
- budget to spend
- measurements
- timelines.

Check 84: Create professional collateral

($) *Medium*   **(🕐)** *Medium–High*

Have your collateral professionally designed and printed. Conduct an internet search to find three agencies that will be able to design your promotional material. You should write a brief document about what you want and need, the type and quantity of products you sell, who your customers are, and the types of promotional information and offers you wish to run. Compare quotes and service levels of each before deciding which is best for your business. Even if you are creating all of the collateral yourself, it's a good idea to write a brief to clearly outline your requirements and stick to your brand message. Remember to include the cost of promotions in your profit and loss spreadsheet, as outlined in check 13.

Getting it done

Now that you have your plan and marketing collateral in place, it's time to start talking to your potential customers.

Check 85: Promote your business

($) *Medium–High* (clock) *Medium–High*

Create a calendar outlining what methods of promotions you will use and when, and note the audience reach. Your calendar should span at least 12 months and could revolve around seasonal events such as spring and Christmas.

Check 86: Measure marketing campaigns

($) *Free* (clock) *Medium–High*

Good marketing is only as good as it is measurable. Ploughing lots of cash into a campaign is pointless if there is no way of measuring the impact on your business. For this reason, as much of your promotion as possible needs to carry a distinct call to action. For example, you could create a new page within your store and direct different promotions to different pages—after you send out your marketing with different URLs, view your traffic reports to gauge the impact. Another call to action could include promoting specific products rather than your overall store.

Check 87: Optimise your marketing plan

 **$ Free–High**   **Medium–High**

> Never rest on your laurels. A good campaign may deliver 5 per cent uplift, for example, but you will never know if it could deliver even more unless you continually optimise your offers, type of collateral, messaging and audience. For this reason, you should never send the same promotion twice but strive to continually learn from your campaigns. Some will definitely fail, but you can learn from these what not to do.

Detailed costs and time for checks 83 to 87

- 1 to 4 weeks to decide on the right marketing agency to help promote your business.

- Marketing costs vary depending on the collateral you choose and in what volumes. You should budget for marketing to be a certain percentage of your sales volume — experiment with how much you can reasonably afford, and the point at which your campaigns start paying back in sales and customers.

Business impact

To gauge potential impact, measure if there's:

- an increase in views (or clicks) to your listings

- an increase in the number of items sold and the number of unique buyers

- an increase in traffic to your eBay store.

More information

Download the marketing plan template from the business.gov.au website at http://goo.gl/oeJSy2.

8

Building for the future

✓ CHECKS 88 TO 90
Set a business goal

What is it?

I once met a successful eBay seller who was turning over $2 million per year. When I asked him what his plans were for the following year he shrugged and said 'I don't know'. What does this tell you about this particular business owner? In short, how can you reach a growth goal if you don't even have one? A reasonable aspirational business goal is often the driver behind successful entrepreneurs. A desire to reach your business goal can help you make tough decisions, and encourage you (and your staff) to try harder.

Three reasons to do it

Setting a business goal or target is a fundamental point of difference between a business owner who is aspirational and future focused, and one who is mired in the day to day of operations.

1 With nothing to aim for it's highly unlikely you will be able to optimise your business operations most effectively.

2 Tracking progress to a business goal is one of the fastest ways to highlight business challenges and opportunities.

3 It's also important to celebrate your successes—if you hit a target, it's worth taking time out to enjoy reaching that milestone.

Getting started

Setting an aspirational but realistic business goal relies upon instinct, assumption *and* knowledge.

Check 88: Create a business goal

$ Free   **Medium–High**

Creating your business goal is arguably the most time-consuming part of this section. You will need to have a thorough understanding of your stock levels, sales prices and competition on eBay. Use a research tool such as Terapeak (www.terapeak.com) to help you gauge the total size of your category on eBay. Look at who the biggest seller is and what their turnover is. How many products do they sell, and how long would it take for you to be the same size, then bigger than them? What realistic percentage of the category could your business own?

Getting it done

A business goal sits within a larger business plan (as covered in check 12). Even operated in isolation, however, it can be invaluable in helping your business grow. A successful goal is as much about market and customer intelligence as it is about keeping you focused and realistic.

Check 89: Measure performance to goal

$ Free   **Medium–High**

Measuring your performance each week and month is critical to getting the most out of your business goal. A sensible business goal has many indicators, including number of buyers, number of sales, sales ratio, average sales prices and number of competitors. As each of these metrics changes, it should impact your tracking against the original goal you set.

Check 90: Review your business goal

$ *Free*   **⏰** *Medium–High*

As with most aspects of running a successful business, your goal is rarely static. Set yourself a calendar reminder and revisit your business goal at least once a quarter to see whether you are on track. If you're exceeding expectations, you could reset the target slightly to ensure you optimise your growth potential—underperformance may encourage you to lower the goal so you can keep morale high. The point here is not to be reactive and continually change your goal, but to remain realistic and responsive to business challenges and opportunities. After all, an impossible goal is as useless as no goal at all.

Detailed costs and time for checks 88 to 90

⏱ 1 to several hours to create a calculated business goal.

$ Setting business goals is cost free.

⏱ About five hours each month to monitor your progress.

Business impact

To gauge potential impact, measure if there's:

(+) an improvement to your turnover expectations

(+) an increase in your profit margins

(+) faster response times to external pressures such as competitors, customers and pricing.

More information

See the *Forbes* guide to successful goal setting at http://goo.gl/38Ttfq.

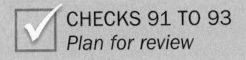

CHECKS 91 TO 93
Plan for review

What is it?

A business is a living, evolving entity. One of the greatest challenges for business owners is to keep reviewing their business's performance even while they are incredibly busy managing day-to-day operations such as fulfilling orders, dealing with suppliers and keeping customers happy. While it's true that these tasks keep the money coming in and bills paid, it cannot be underestimated how crucial regular reviews are. In some instances, it may even be more sensible to pause day-to-day operations rather than continue to operate in a manner that is not as profitable as planned or is not achieving business goals. The important thing to remember is to keep concentrating on the big picture — how is my business performing overall?

Three reasons to do it

Operating a successful business is about having your finger on its pulse — at all times. Losing focus or failing to keep informed is a sure-fire way to lose track of opportunities for, and threats to, growth.

1 Quickly identify changing trends and readjust your business's operations to avoid major issues.

2 Complete administrative tasks such as tax returns, BAS (business activity statements) and supplier negotiations faster.

3 Carve out time for review at the beginning of the year, before you are consumed with the day-to-day running operations of your business.

Getting started

The first step in planning for review is just that—ensuring you have allocated the appropriate amount of time to sit down and review your business.

Check 91: Set a review reminder ($) Free (🕐) Low

Create a calendar reminder for a business review each quarter. This should be a minimum of three hours on a day and in a location where you will be free from interruption. Set yourself clear guidelines, such as no telephone and no appointments. It's sensible also to set yourself a reminder two days before the review so you can avoid scheduling conflicts.

Getting it done

Reviewing your business will take time and require ready access to the relevant information.

Check 92: Review business performance

($) Free (🕐) High

Have all of your operating rhythms documented and well ordered. The easiest way is to use your computer to save all of the information—you could consider a third-party program such as MYOB (myob.com.au). Information you will need includes:

- profit and loss spreadsheet
- customer information (details, comments, orders)
- eBay information (fees, upcoming changes and so on)
- eBay reporting (sales reports, traffic reports, invoices and so on)
- current stock levels
- supplier details and terms
- other providers' details and terms.

Check 93: Trending business performance

$ Free   Medium–High

> Reviewing your business is mainly about highlighting data trends—both good and bad. The easiest way to assess the trend is to compare it with the previous three months. What has changed, by how much and why? You can download business review plans from the internet (see more information below).

Detailed costs and time for checks 91 to 93

- 3 to several hours each quarter to review your business in great detail.
- 1 to 3 hours each quarter to write an action plan to adjust your operating rhythms.
- Several days to implement your review plan.
- It costs nothing but time to review your business, but you may wish to consider asking an external party to conduct the review for you. This is likely to be more objective and could be faster, but may cost thousands of dollars.

Business impact

To gauge potential impact, measure if there's:

- (+) an increase in your overall sales volume
- (+) an increase in your profit margin.

More information

View the Queensland government's business performance guidelines at http://goo.gl/hdOOj8.

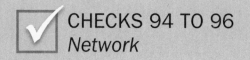

CHECKS 94 TO 96
Network

What is it?

Networking with other eBay sellers and eCommerce business owners is one of the most effective ways of learning and improving your business. Throughout the year there are opportunities for you to meet professional eBay business sellers and ask them about their own journeys and successes. Naturally there will be some aspects of business that are closely guarded secrets (such as suppliers and profit margins), but most eBay sellers are happy to share their advice and learn about your own experiences. Choosing the right event here is critical, because you don't have the luxury of wasting your time at events that give you no clear actions to implement within your business. Most events also include exhibitors whose services are relevant to your business; often investing in a third-party solution can help you boost turnover and improve profits.

Three reasons to do it

Learning from experienced professionals is one of the most effective ways of expanding your skills and improving your business's performance.

1 Networking challenges your own perceptions and encourages you to be more objective in assessing your business and its challenges and opportunities.

2 Networking can lead to additional business opportunities such as expanding your range.

3 Sharing your knowledge can be personally fulfilling and rewarding.

Getting started

There are countless conferences and events that you can attend each year. Inevitably they are a little hit-and-miss, and you need to take some time to find the ones that are likely to provide you with the best business insights and most effective business contacts. Avoid those with hefty registration fees and those that appear to be inundated with businesses trying to pitch their services to you. Look specifically for events with clearly allocated networking time.

Check 94: Research networking events

 $ *Free* **🕐** *Low–Medium*

Spend a few hours on the internet searching for some networking events to attend. These do not have to be in-person events; some may be online events or forums.

Check 95: Register for networking events

$ *Free–Medium* **🕐** *Low–High*

Aim for at least three per year. Register for one online forum (consider eBay's forums at http://goo.gl/dvtr7o), one in-person event (consider the annual Internet Conference at www.internetconference.com.au) and another event you find appealing.

Getting it done

Merely registering for and attending an event is not enough, however! You need to plan to get the most out of them.

Check 96: Set event targets

$ Free–Medium   **Low–High**

> For each event, set yourself a goal to meet a minimum number of people and collect a minimum number of contacts. You could also aim to secure at least one ongoing business mentor from each event. Be prepared to take notes and ensure you collect at least three BIG ideas for your business, then implement each within one month of the event.

Detailed costs and time for checks 94 to 96

- In-person events can take from 1 to 3 days, depending on location and agenda.
- Ticket prices for the Internet Conference are usually less than $1000.
- It is free to use most online forums, including eBay's.

Business impact

To gauge potential impact, measure if there's:

- a new idea (or ideas) to help improve your eBay business's turnover or profit margin
- an ongoing network of business supporters who are available to answer your questions.

More information

For more information about the Internet Conference visit http://goo.gl/zIzN2q.

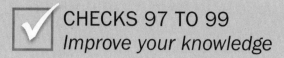

CHECKS 97 TO 99
Improve your knowledge

What is it?

Nearly every business owner I have met has told me there simply isn't enough time in the day to do everything associated with running a business. One of the things that often suffers as a result is the business owner's own knowledge. In this case, knowledge of industry and marketplace trends is one thing, but technological advances, eBay product updates and government regulations are quite another. With the wealth of information available, the important thing is to concentrate on quality, not quantity, of information.

Three reasons to do it

1 Responding to upcoming change before it happens will save you time, resources and stress in the future.

2 Gain a competitive advantage over other business owners who do not allocate time to comprehend trends and changes within your category.

3 Expanded knowledge can lead to new business opportunities and growth.

Getting started

Be firm with yourself and ensure you stick to your plan of trying to expand your knowledge frequently.

Check 97: Set knowledge reminder ($) Free (clock) Low

Set yourself a calendar reminder to set aside one hour each week. It should be at the same time on the same day so you get into the habit of using this hour to expand your business knowledge. Ensure the hour is free from interruptions.

Getting it done

Keep your knowledge about eBay and your industry current.

Check 98: Learn more about eBay

($) Free–Low (clock) Low–Medium

One area of knowledge to expand is eBay itself. The site is continually being updated and often requires sellers to adjust their business practices. Ensure you read every communication you receive from eBay (you could create a new folder in your inbox and read these during your knowledge hour each week) and always check the News area of the site to look for updates at http://goo.gl/OmMi8l.

Check 99: Learn more about eCommerce

($) Free–Low (clock) Low–Medium

Conduct an internet search to find a blog, newsletter or other website relevant to eBay selling, your industry or eCommerce. Sign up to receive emails automatically and save these to read during your knowledge hour each week. Alternatively, you could subscribe to a magazine or ebooks.

Detailed costs and time for checks 97 to 99

⊕ 1 hour each week to read the information.

⑤ Subscribing to most email services is free; however, magazines and other websites may charge a small monthly subscription fee.

Business impact

To gauge potential impact, measure if there's:

⊕ an improvement in the efficiency of your business operations

⊖ a decrease in the number of changes to the eBay site that come as a surprise.

More information

Consider the Professional eBay and eCommerce Sellers Alliance blog at http://goo.gl/qK7JpK.

✓ CHECK 100
Conclusion

You can't make a million dollars in your sleep. Running any business requires careful planning, constant re-evaluation and close monitoring. To be successful on eBay you need to be able to cut through the daily grind and implement those changes or tactics that will provide the biggest cut-through — you need to increase your turnover, drive down your costs and see your profit margin increase. Be careful, however, not to obsess about the margin. I've seen too many sellers lose sleep over 0.5 per cent when what they should have been doing was focusing on the volume of cash profit. After all, selling 10 fifteen-dollar products at a 50 per cent margin nets you $75, whereas selling 1000 five-dollar products at a 10 per cent margin nets you $500.

Today, business owners are expected to be jacks of all trades. You have to find time to plan your business, run your business, satisfy customers and, if you're like me, pack your products and drive them to the post office, and follow up on customer satisfaction. Time is of the essence and one of the most overlooked but critical components of business success is reducing your time investment so your virtual hourly rate is optimised.

Check 100 is your toolbox for streamlining your eBay business. You can troubleshoot or else pick a page at random and apply the lessons to your operations. Some of the checks are fast, free and simple; others may take longer and may force you outside your comfort zone, but that's all part of running a profitable and long-term successful business, whether on eBay or not.

Now that you have completed 99 checks, there's only one thing to do. Go back and check again, because no business can afford to rest on its laurels. The most successful are continually reinventing themselves and challenging their ways of working. One hundred checks a year could be the only thing that lifts you from a mediocre result to one that far exceeds your profit expectation.

Check 100: Now go back and start all over again!

Learn more with practical advice from our experts

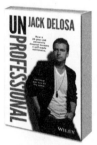